history of a landscape

Sydney

Françoise Fromonot
Christopher Thompson

history of a landscape
Sydney

VILO

PUBLISHING

Title page illustration
The centre of Sydney seen from Shark Beach at Vaucluse Point on the eastern side of the harbour.

Contents

G. W. Evans, *A View of Sydney New South Wales, on entering the Heads, the distance seven miles*, about 1795.

Introduction

Since its foundation by the British in 1788 – who established a penal colony in a country they regarded as uninhabited – Sydney has been a place of intrigue for the rest of the world. Opinions of the city have varied over the years: a hotbed of vice and corruption, an earthly paradise surrounding the most beautiful harbour in the world, a great seaport, the site of one of the monuments of modern architecture, the Sydney Opera House, a vast sprawling suburb bedecked with a fringe of extraordinary beaches. Contradictory and unpredictable, Sydney is a vital testament to the dilemmas of the society that constructed it, from the humble origins of the first European settlement (one thousand Britons, ten thousand bricks and a stack of pamphlets urging the felons to chastity, all thrown together into an environment possessed of every beauty nature could provide) to the dynamic, multicultural, hedonistic city of four million people – now the largest in Australia – selected to host the 27th Olympiad.

This book is an account of Sydney seen through a history of its architecture and landscape. Neither history, architecture nor landscape are terms that had meaning in Australia prior to the arrival of the British at the end of the eighteenth century. Thus this book is about the impact of an alien cultural phenomenon – the city – on an indigenous environment. Sydney is one of the few major cities in the world that has been documented – through maps, paintings, drawings, memoirs and reports – from the very moment of its birth. From the beginning, landscape has played a significant role in the imagination of the city's inhabitants and on its overall development. Acquiring knowledge of natural phenomena was a key feature of the exploration of the South Pacific by the scientists of the eighteenth century Enlightenment. Early accounts of the settlement focus on the overwhelming nature of the native landscape, its novelty, its difference to that found in the then known world and, not least, its astonishingly pristine beauty. Two hundred odd years later, the landscape remains the dominant element in the city's appearance, a source of inspiration for more innovative contemporary architects; a pretext for those responsible for the development of the city's urban form. In its bid to hold the Olympic Games, Sydney bound itself to the idea of sustainable environmental development, opted to become a laboratory of urban experiment and envisaged itself as a city deferring to its landscape and climate. The outcome of this bold move remains uncertain – and will be so for some time but it allows the possibility that Sydney – for so long a borrower of architectural and urban models – will endow the world with the consequences of this experiment.

What are often perceived as examples of Australian architecture, both nationally and internationally, are buildings designed, more often than not, in the currently fashionable architectural language of Sydney: "open-ended, lightweight architecture", one claiming to be informed by place and climate, one seeking to define a unique identity. This quest for identity has been a driving force behind much of the architectural and urban development of a city established primarily to house the overflow of British penal justice. During the nineteenth century Sydney sought to model itself as an antipodean Britain, denying its social and geographical context; a curious inversion of the political and cultural phenomena occurring contemporaneously in much of Europe and America. The twentieth century has seen these same passions channelled in a search to determine a uniquely Australian, or more pertinently, a specifically Sydney position in the face of an increasingly international world. Even in 2000, Sydney is some twenty-two hours flying time from Europe, eleven from North America; Australians still are wont to describe themselves as being isolated from the world. Ironically, the very concept of an "uniquely Australian architecture" reflects quintessentially Anglo-Saxon attitudes; an empirical belief that national character results from an environment – by this definition a combination of landscape and climate – inhabited by a sturdy, practical and democratic populace. It is a stance underpinned by a distrust of theory; a belief that it is essential to experience something before it can be perceived as true.

These are some of the paradoxes that define the architecture and the urban fabric of Sydney today: in pragmatic terms "open-ended, lightweight architecture" is no more valid a response to its sub-tropical climate than enclosure and mass. The contemporary passion for an architecture of the environment – for preserving the native landscape intact – has turned bushland into suburbia, albeit an exclusive one. This self-proclaimed multicultural society has little architecture other than that derived from the dominant cultures of Western Europe and North America. And this declaredly free and open democracy accepts, almost without question, an authoritarian management of its public architecture and planning, one notably lacking transparency and genuine public accountability. A blend of laissez-faire attitude and periodic outbursts of control and regulation is characteristic of the way Sydney has dealt with issues of architecture and planning since its foundation. Our book sets out to explore some of these dilemmas.

Satellite view of Sydney, January 2000. Bordered by national parks
to the north and south, the city stretches some one hundred kilometres west to the Blue Mountains.

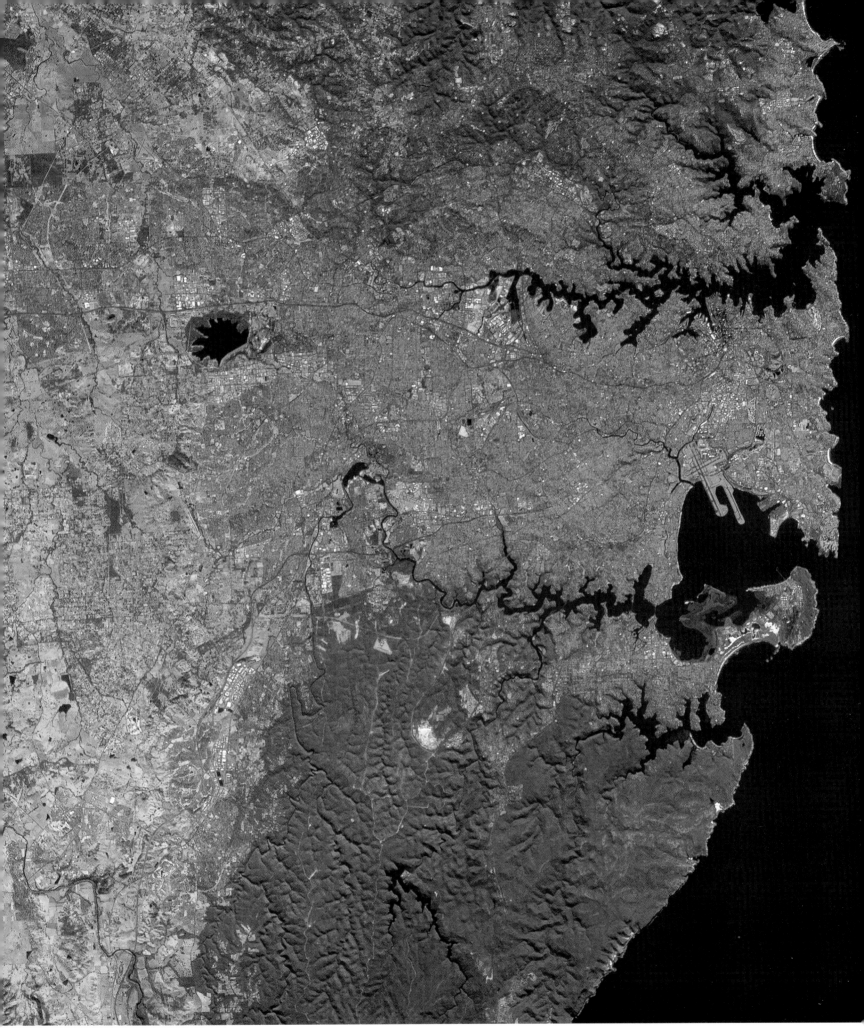

Sketch & Description of the Settlement at **SYDNEY COVE PORT JACKSON** in the **COUNTY** of **CUMBERLAND** taken

by a transported Convict on the 16th of April, 1788. which was not quite 3 Months after Commodore Phillips's landing there

Sydney Cove lies 3 Leagues to the Northward of **BOTANY BAY** which is situated in Lat.34.S: Long.151 E.

Sketch & Description of the Settlement at Sydney Cove Port Jackson …, after Joseph Fowkes, 1789.

Beginnings

Ab origine

A vast, open plateau of scrub-covered sandstone crowned by clumps of eucalyptus forest, mounted above precipitous cliffs and wrapped around a broad, clefted, harbour of idyllic appearance: such was the place soon to be Sydney, prior to the arrival of the Europeans in 1788. Watkin Tench, one of the first Britons to set sight on the place, observed that: "The first impression made on a stranger is certainly favourable. He sees gently swelling hills connected by vales which possess every beauty that verdure of trees, and form, simply considered in itself, can produce."[1] Ignoring James Cook's observation of the presence of inhabitants along the coast he explored in 1770, the instructions given to Arthur Phillip – the commander of the fleet carrying the first colonists – by the authorities in Britain presumed a state of *terra nullius* – an empty land.[2] To those forming part of that dismal body – the first fleet – evidence contrary to these presumptions was provided on arrival by the local inhabitants of the area, speculatively disdainful and apprehensive of the upholstered, pink-skinned men and women in large vessels who had appeared in their midst. For their part the British colonists deprived the local Aboriginals, the Eora, of their land, their livelihood and, ultimately, their existence. At first the Aboriginals were observed as natural history specimens: the social habits, weapons, tools and structures of the tribes who inhabited the area around Port Jackson were recorded in journals and as fugitive images in the topographical drawings and paintings of the Europeans. Later they would be used and discarded by the authorities in much the same manner as the convicts whose transportation to the continent was the operative rationale behind white invasion. The European obsession with shelter, with the moral "respectability of bricks and mortar"[3] was of little consequence to those who lived within nature rather than as intruders amongst or against it. The "noble savage" of Enlightenment thought was, in terms of the pragmatic reasoning of the British authorities, no more than a philosophical conceit.[4]

In a legal sense the European settlement of Sydney began on 7 February 1788 at Sydney Cove[5] with the proclamation of Arthur Phillip as governor and captain-general of the British penal colony of New South Wales. This ceremony occurred twelve days after the arrival in Port Jackson of over one thousand Britons (seven hundred and fifty-nine of them convicts) in eleven ships. The site envisaged for settlement was Botany Bay, a location selected by the British authorities

William Bradley, *Sydney Cove, Port Jackson*, 1788.

Arthur Bowes Smyth, *A View of the Tree at Botany Bay which yields ye Yellow Balsam, & of a Wigwam*, 1788. An early European record of an Aboriginal shelter.

Convict Settlement

on the basis of glowing reports made by Cook and his politically-influential botanist Joseph Banks. Arriving at Botany Bay on 19 January 1788 they found the reality strikingly different from the reports; it was a sandy, swamp-filled wasteland, "very open and greatly exposed to the fury of the south-east winds", with minimal supplies of potable water. Phillip immediately dispatched an exploration party to nearby Port Jackson. The seamen returned "with such an account of the harbour and advantages attending the place" that Phillip decided to transfer the place of settlement immediately. His decision was reinforced the following day by the surprise arrival of two French ships, the *Boussole* and *Astrolabe* on an exploratory mission under the command of Jean-François de La Pérouse; in the aftermath of the revolution in North America he was perhaps apprehensive that the French too, wished to colonise the continent. After an exchange of civilities the British decamped to Port Jackson where, as Phillip Gidley King, second lieutenant on Phillip's ship, the *Sirius* recollected: "The next Morning Jany 27th A great part of the Troops & Convicts were landed, & the latter was immediately sett to work clearing away the ground, ready for the encampment. The Place on which the settlement is to be made is at the head of a Cove at the head of which a small rivulet empties it self. The shore on each side is bounded by rocks, within which there is a very fine soil & full of trees which will require some time & labour to clear away, the Marines & Convicts are to be encamped on the West side & the Governor, & Staff with his guard & a small part of the Convicts on the East side of the Rivulet."[6]

Phillip had been instructed to use his discretion in the layout of the settlement. His initial

New South Wales View of Sydney from the East Side of the Cove, No 1 & No 2, after John Eyre. Published in D. D. Mann, *Present Picture of New South Wales*, London, 1811.

actions aimed at separating the various groups under his command into manageable units; he had hoped earlier to find a site bisected by a river in order to isolate the guards from the guarded.[7] Such wishes were dashed by the piddling reality of the Tank Stream that drained into the Cove. Nonetheless, he ordered William Dawes to draw up a plan for the future township; a project that was axial, symmetrical and consciously symbolic of authority with its origins rooted in Baroque vista planning as found, for example, in the layout of the Royal Naval Hospital at Greenwich.[8] With a sense of irony, given the meagre actuality of life at Sydney Cove, Tench observed that: "To proceed on a narrow, confined scale, in a country of the extensive limits we possess, would be unpardonable: extent of empire demands grandeur of design."[9] But despite attempts to maintain Crown control over the layout and to enforce restrictions on the extent of settlement, Sydney's pattern of streets evolved in an ad hoc, almost medieval manner, from an ordered military encampment into a messy village. The negative logic underpinning this growth was, as ever, a deficiency of resources and the short-term prospect of easy gain. Phillip's design for a neatly arranged settlement of civilised people, part of a vast British empire, never materialised, although his idea of differentiating the functional from the administrative components of the settlement defined Sydney's future development. In general terms the western part became commercial and industrial whilst its eastern flank was characterised by open spaces and, eventually, genteel suburbs.

The first storehouses were constructed of brick and weatherboard. Ten thousand bricks were sent with the fleet along with tools, brick moulds and window glass. The huts for convicts and Marines alike were "built of Posts stuck in the Ground at convenient distances

Juan Ravanet, *Borador del Resiviemento de los Oficiales en baia Botanica (Meeting of the officials at Botany Bay)*, 1793. It shows the verandah attached to the Lieutenant Governor's House.

ador del Reenviamiento Delos Oficiales in me Bl

to support Wattles and plastered both inside & out."[10] Roofs were thatched with rushes, later covered with she-oak shingles after rushes proved inadequate to the penetrating vigour of the Sydney rain; for this reason the temporary hospital had to be replaced in June 1790 by a prefabricated "Military moveable hospital." The foundation stone for Government House, the first permanent house in the colony, was laid four months after the arrival of the Europeans; it was to last until 1845 in modified form.[11] Rising over the huddle of crumbling huts it was a symbolic reminder of the authority of the governor, evoking stability and providing a level of domestic comfort denied to the greater part of the population. In December 1792 Phillip returned to Britain having nurtured a brief flowering of public building. Those government structures raised over the next eighteen years – such as the new prison erected at Sydney Cove in 1797 – consolidated his original plans. The second governor, John Hunter, whilst advocating an ambitious building programme found his efforts curtailed by a lack of manpower. In constructing new prisons and a new church, St Phillip's, he was driven to impose levies of labour or cash to ensure completion. Superseding the temporary huts, buildings of a vernacular type dominated construction in the settlement for many years. A drawing made during the visit of a Spanish expedition in 1793 records low, eaveless, gable-roofed whitewashed brick cottages. Looming over them on the western ridge are the barracks (1789) and the uncut bush. The focus of the drawing is the lieutenant governor's house (1788). Five years after its construction this stone cottage had been embellished with the colony's first verandah. In terms of a British vernacular tradition the verandah was an alien element; frequently used by Europeans in India, Sri Lanka, the Dutch East Indies and the Caribbean, it was becoming a fashionable feature in North America and Britain at the beginning of the nineteenth century. But, despite the aptness of this innovation to the climate, its use in Sydney was limited at first to official buildings: an 1805 notice in the *Sydney Gazette* advertised a contract for the construction of a court house, specifying "a Varando in front, with a small room at each end"[12] – a prototype, that in a domestic guise became a standard form of building during the nineteenth century – the Australian colonial bungalow.[13]

In spite of British efforts to establish the settlement as a place of dread and punishment, trade inevitably arose. Wealth and the pursuit of social status were sought by convict and guard alike, so prestigious buildings were seen as proper adjuncts to such ambitions. In 1793 John Macarthur, a lieutenant in the New South Wales Corps, using monies derived from his trading ventures began constructing such a building, Elizabeth Farm, on property granted to him at Parramatta, 18 kilometres west of Sydney Cove. Macarthur had a passion for architecture and he was to indulge in it over the next forty-one years. Elizabeth Farm, the first of his schemes, is the earliest surviving building in Sydney.[14] Hunter's successors, Phillip Gidley King and William Bligh, saw no need to enrich the settlement with public architecture. Except that the irascible Bligh, that pertinacious survivor of the *Bounty* mutiny, attempted to pull the settlement into ship-shape order by enforcing Phillip's by now redundant town plan. He queried the validity of a number of the town leases and ordered illegal occupants of property to move. His planning actions were a contributing factor in the Rum Rebellion of 1807 which saw him deposed ignominiously by members of the New South Wales Corps acting under the thrall of colonial notables such as Macarthur. Thus twenty-one years after its foundation, the British penal settlement at Sydney Cove had evolved into a small sea port, one trafficking not only in convicts but also in wool, the products of whaling and sealing and the general commerce of a pioneering settlement with incipient hopes of greater things to come. It was, as the administrators in Whitehall would have wished it to be, mutinies notwithstanding: a convenient receptacle for the victims of British justice, and in practical terms, one increasingly self-supporting.

The arrest of Governor Bligh in Government House during the "Rum Rebellion."
It is the earliest known view of a Sydney interior. Unknown artist, 1809.

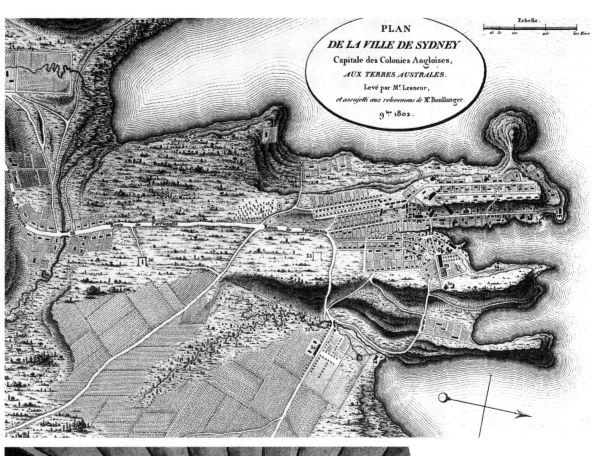

The Colonial Town

Francis Greenway, *Self portrait*, about 1810, prior to his arrival in Sydney as a convict.

Top:

Richard Read senior, *Lachlan Macquarie Esqre, Feb. 11 1822.* A valedictory record of a popular governor.

The arrival of the new governor Lachlan Macquarie, his wife Elizabeth and her pattern books on 28 December 1809 changed Sydney from being a small settlement of no architectural distinction to a sizeable town of some architectural pretension. Macquarie justified the ambitious public building program he set into motion by observing that on his arrival "all was in a most ruinous state of decay." He was a soldier, his wife a scion of the minor Scottish gentry and the pattern books that can be identified were compiled by the English architect Edward Gyfford.[15] As well, these architectural amateurs brought with them memories of buildings not only from "home" but also from the Carribean and India. Their eagerness for change was impressive; in just over a year following their accession the couple's untutored taste for dog-Palladian architecture found form in the three buildings forming the Sydney General Hospital; their appearance is generally believed to have been based on that of the Government House at Madras. Functional considerations aside the hospital was intended as a mark of picturesque gentility, a statement of gubernatorial authority set on the eastern ridges of Sydney. So taken by the success of his venture, Macquarie later erected a similar structure – the Military Hospital – on the western side of the town.[16]

Pattern books aside, the great obstacle encountered by the Macquaries in realising a vision for their demesne was that their ambitions exceeded both their taste and the pool of architectural talent found in New South Wales. As with their predecessors they relied on the utilitarian skills of military engineers and convict builders. In April 1817 Macquarie advised his superior in London that: "From the want of a Scientific Person to Plan and Superintend the Construction of all Government Public Buildings, most of them have hitherto been very badly planned and still worse Executed – a man named Francis Howard Greenway, who came out here a Convict in the Year 1814, and who was originally an Architect of some Eminence in England, having been strongly recommended to me by the late Governor Phillip, I have availed myself of his Skill and Scientific Knowledge as a Civil Architect, and accordingly sometime since Employed him to act in that capacity ... this man is extremely useful."[17] Born in 1777 into a family of builders, masons, quarrymen and architects, Greenway trained as an architect in Bristol and London – with John Nash – before returning home to establish a practice in Bristol. He was declared bankrupt in 1809 and was subsequently convicted on a charge of forgery; his death sentence being commuted into transportation to Botany Bay. Greenway's first scheme as civil architect was a lighthouse at South Head. Dramatically positioned above the harbour entrance it acted as a signpost to the remote settlement, a picturesque terminus to the untamed landscape and a symbol of totemic significance to the inhabitants of the colony. The partnership between Macquarie and Greenway during these halcyon days resulted in an impressive number of public buildings including, notably, the Hyde Park Barracks (1817) and St. James's Church (1820).[18] More was planned including a new Government House, an Anglican cathedral surrounded by a "Great Square" and an ambitious layout for Sydney's rambling streets. Greenway's designs complemented the unsophisticated tastes of the governor and his wife. His architecture was formulaic, provincial Palladian, and its realisation benefited from an increasing supply of convict labour as, in the period following the cessation of the Napoleonic Wars in 1815, the white population of the colony grew from under 13,000 to 30,000 by 1821.

Reports of a megalomaniac building spree along with shifts in the demography of the population – free settlers now began to outnumber convicts – prompted the British government into setting up a commission of inquiry into the governance of the colony.

Joseph Lycett, *Convict Barracks, Hyde Park*, about 1820.
Greenway's 1817 barracks in the guise of an English
provincial Palladian barn.

Augustus Earle, *Sydney Lighthouse*, 1826.
Greenway's first scheme for Macquarie (1817).

General Hospital, Sydney (1811). Macquarie's "dog Palladian"
hospital was financed and built through the sale of a rum
monopoly. Unknown photographer, about 1870.

Richard Read junior, *Elizabeth Henrietta Villa Situate about four miles down the harbour from Sydney Cove the seat of John Piper Esq.r Naval Officer &c of Port Jackson New South Wales, 1820.* Henrietta Villa was the short-lived Henry Kitchen's principal work.

Its outcome saw the Macquaries recalled from their prison settlement estate, Greenway dismissed and public architecture abandoned until the colony began to take control of its own affairs in the late 1830s. The British government, acutely conscious as to the costs of building,[19] proscribed official expenditure on architecture other than where it was used to house and secure convicts: " ... transportation to New South Wales is intended as a severe punishment ... and as such must be rendered an object of real terror to all classes of the community."[20]

By 1816 Greenway was no longer the only architect of more than passing competence in Sydney. Henry Kitchen, a former pupil of James Wyatt, arrived as a settler and attracted a small but prestigious clientele including John Piper, the colony's naval officer and leader of its social set. For this paragon he designed Henrietta Villa at Point Piper (1816),[21] credited as the most sophisticated house in New South Wales. Kitchen's work for Macarthur, the "great perturbator", was equally significant, even if little was built. Despite Macarthur's extended absences overseas he had visions of using his tenaciously acquired wealth to create a residence suitable to his status. Kitchen was employed by Macarthur on projects for a mansion at Pyrmont and for his properties at Elizabeth Farm including Hambledon Cottage and the Home Farm at Camden Park.[22] But architecture was not a factor in the majority of buildings raised in Sydney during the boom years of the 1820s; these were erected by builders responding to the simple need for shops, houses, inns, churches,

Campbell Lane: cheaply constructed worker's housing
erected in Surry Hills from 1833, by John Nobbs
and John Brown. Unknown photographer, about 1880.

Elizabeth Bay House designed in 1832 by John Verge for
the Colonial Secretary Alexander Macleay. Photographed
with its garden still intact about 1890.

factories and warehouses. This boom was a response not only to population growth but also to government concessions aimed at encouraging free trade and agricultural exports and the advent of perpetual leases on town properties. In the late 1820s landowners at the southern end of the town began subdividing properties for gentlemen's residences and in 1833 into narrow allotments for rented working class housing.[23] The buildings erected on these nine to twenty foot (2.75 to 6 metres) wide lots, were rudimentary, unwatered and unsewered, some two storied "one up one down" terraces, many merely wooden cottages. In twenty years time they would be described as slums, yet housing of this type continued to be built until well into the 1870s.

Private development again was behind Sydney's first genteel suburb on Woolloomooloo Hill — now Pott's Point — but it was the will of the governor Ralph Darling and his architecturally inclined wife that made it possible. Over a seven year period a number of villas were erected for "respectable" persons over this rocky promontory, notably by John Verge who had worked as a builder in London for over twenty years before migrating in 1828. He had a ready market for his skills building cottages, houses including terraces and at least one prefabricated house,[24] a hotel, shop fronts and an addition to St. James's church. But it seems that the colonial elite employed him more for his skills as a capable builder than as a designer.[25] Verge provided his clients with "elegant houses, well scaled, competently built and embellished with beautifully designed and resolved Greek Revival

Mortimer Lewis with an elevation of what is probably his 1849 Colonial Treasury building. Unknown Daguerreotypist, about 1855.

detailing."[26] By 1835 he had built a possible eight villas and a cottage on Woolloomooloo Hill including the elegant but unfinished Elizabeth Bay House for the colonial secretary Alexander Macleay.[27] Three of the villas designed by Verge remain, albeit in restored states and in much truncated urban settings: Tusculum (designed 1830, built from 1832) is now occupied by the Royal Australian Institute of Architects; Rockwall (designed 1830 and built by 1837); Elizabeth Bay House (designed 1832) is now an historic house museum. And in 1831 Macarthur employed Verge to realise his villa at Camden Park outside Sydney, ending a decades-long quest to give built form to his achievements. In response to this evolving urbanism a series of proclamations and acts were introduced during the 1830s aimed at regulating uncontrolled development in Sydney. The 1838 *Act for Regulating Buildings and Party-Walls, and for Preventing Mischiefs by Fire, in the Town of Sydney* signalled the end of vernacular building within the confines of the town and increased the density of housing. Not least, these laws gave property real, convertible value. The possession of bricks and mortar was no longer primarily an attribute of "moral respectability", it was commodity. And although passed by the appointed local legislature, these acts constitute the Colonial Office's last attempts to control the town's growth and development.

By 1837 at least fourteen architects are known to have been practicing in New South Wales. They served a population of 77,000 of whom 20,000 lived in Sydney and, for the greater part, their work remains anonymous. Among them were John Bibb whose commissions included the Congregational Church (1840) – "the handsomest building of the kind in Sydney" – in Pitt Street and James Hume who designed the nave of St Andrew's Cathedral (1837), condemned soon after as "an epitome of all that is commonplace"[28] along with a bizarre Egyptian revival synagogue (1835). Destitute and all but forgotten, Greenway died in 1837. Classicism remained the dominant style for public works: George Barney, the commanding Royal Engineer, used it for the 1841 convict barracks on Cockatoo Island and for the Victoria Barracks in Paddington. Mortimer Lewis, colonial architect from 1835 to 1849, designed the Darlinghurst Courthouse (1844), the Customs House (1844), the Colonial Treasury (1849) and the Australian Museum (1846-54)[29] in this architectural language but in a variant that had little to do with Greenway's eighteenth century Palladianism. His was a consciously modern classicism, drawing on precedents developed in Britain by the like of Smirke and Barry, even if it suffered from want of comparison in its colonial translation.

The boom years of the late 1830s, fuelled by agricultural revenues, ready finance from colonial banks and a freeing up of land titles, galvanised a wave of speculative building: terraced housing on the English pattern, villas and town houses, banks, churches and hotels rose out of the rubble of the prison-settlement town. The cessation of transportation in 1840, the establishment of an elected Legislative Council in 1841 and an increasing flow of settlers all contributed to an atmosphere of frenzied building. But between 1841 and 1844 it came to a grinding halt, just as Sydney was incorporated as a city in 1842. Property values plummeted and undercapitalised speculators recoiled as banks tried to limit their exposure to this financial debacle. The governor fared better: at the end of 1832 Whitehall approved the construction of a new government house.

Having little faith in local architects, the governor Richard Bourke requested that designs be prepared by "some eminent architect in London." The colonial agent selected Edward Blore, an architect better known for the reasonableness of his costs than for his genius as a designer. He had little knowledge of Sydney – his drawings are labelled "Governor's House, Sidney" – and was poorly briefed as to the different climatic conditions to be encountered in the colony. Blore's design, incorporating elements of Gothic, Elizabethan

George Peacock, *Supreme Court House Sydney NSW, 1845*. As a symbol of the crown's penitential powers, the court house was Lewis's most potent design.

George Peacock, *Sydney from Kirribilli Point*, 1851.
The whitened sepulchres of Edward Blore's Government House (1835) dominating Sydney Cove, Fort Macquarie (1815) below.

Opposite page, top:

George Peacock, *Sydney from Woolloomooloo*, 1849. The gradual urban infiltration of the still spectacular natural landscape.

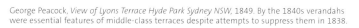

George Peacock, *View of Lyons Terrace Hyde Park Sydney NSW*, 1849. By the 1840s verandahs were essential features of middle-class terraces despite attempts to suppress them in 1838.

J. H. Jones, *Circular Quay in 1845*, Lewis's recently completed Customs House marked the start of intensive development of the south-east of the Cove, an area previously reserved for the governor.

Campbell's Wharf, Sydney Cove, about 1870, by an unknown photographer. The buildings in the foreground largely pre-date the 1850s, but in the background Barnet's Colonial Secretary's Office has altered the landscape irretrievably.

and Moorish styles, was a metropolitan "grammar of ornament" made tangible, a three-dimensional compendium of his stylistic preferences. Building began in 1837, under the supervision of Lewis, and was completed in 1845.[30] The writer Joseph Fowles observed that "altogether, it is one of the most imposing buildings we have; and whether viewed from the adjacent Domain, the harbour, or the City, its tall chimneys of elaborately carved stone, white turrets and numerous windows, render it a conspicuous ornament to our metropolis."[31] Blore's building gave new blood to the Gothic in Sydney, and its wealthier inhabitants were quick to adopt a style which made the links to "home" evident and reinforced connections with the British lordlings sent out to govern New South Wales. The style was also deemed appropriate for the Anglican Church. Shortly after immigrating in 1842 Edmund Blacket was appointed diocesan architect. He embarked on a programme of church building, all in the Gothic style.[32] Blacket replaced Lewis as colonial architect after the latter's resignation following a politically inspired investigation into his costing of the Australian Museum.

The landscape in which these buildings were set was still, clearly, a native one, no matter how like England its inhabitants might wish it to be. Attempts in 1832 by the surveyor general Thomas Mitchell to lay out the city on a grid pattern, one that ignored not only the contours of the terrain but also private property, had largely fallen afoul

Observatory Hill and the entrance to Darling Harbour seen from Pyrmont. Photographed by John Smith, about 1860.

Blacket's Gothic university building from its quadrangle, designed in imitation of Christ Church, Oxford. Photographed by John Smith, about 1860.

of the vested interests of landowners,[33] although in the newer, inner-city suburbs a pattern of rectilinear streets was emerging. And architecture in Sydney was no longer embraced simply in order to raise a building's occupant above the common herd; it was now a matter of civic interest that the newly incorporated city be perceived outside its bounds as no longer the depository of convicts, the dumping ground of British justice. Sydney wanted to be seen to be as much like the motherland as was possible: the illusion could be sustained by adopting a medieval European style, the "English national style", one imbued with the moral authority of church and state, even if it was an idiom inappropriate both to the society and the semi-tropical climate of this new land.

The Colonial City

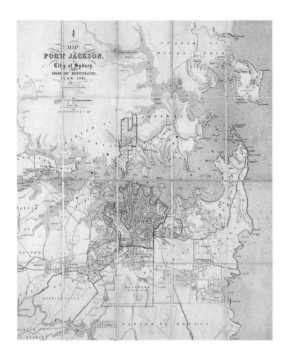

J. A. C. Willis, *Map of Port Jackson and City of Sydney showing the Adjacent Municipalities, NSW, 1865.*

In 1850 the Legislative Council of New South Wales passed an act for the establishment of a university at Sydney. Anticipated by the Colonial Office as far back as 1823, the university was to prepare colonists for the higher levels of political and civil service and to safeguard professional standards. Its motto "*Sidere mens eadem mutato* (the mind remains the same no matter the place)" reflected an unquestioning attachment to Britain; the Gothic style adopted for its buildings was, equally, transparently genuflectory. Built between 1854 and 1862 to the design of Blacket, who resigned from his post as colonial architect in order to undertake the scheme, it marked the beginning of a new era for not only the society it served but also in the way its public buildings were regarded; from being functional manifestations of imperial power they now had to reflect the status of the city itself. The same year saw the Port Phillip District separated from New South Wales to form the colony of Victoria. In 1851 gold was discovered near Bathurst in the backblocks of New South Wales; a serendipitous find, surpassed soon after when a larger strike was made in Victoria. Over the next century Sydney lost its financial preeminence to Melbourne, yet from being a city of some 50,000 persons in 1851 it grew to nearly 100,000 in the course of the decade and by 1891 it had reached 400,000, three quarters of whom lived in suburbs.[34] Most importantly, in 1856, New South Wales became self-governing, and the focus of patronage moved from the colonial authorities in Britain, represented in the person of the governor and his civil service advisers, to those individuals chosen for office by a local electorate. Sydney's development over the second half of the nineteenth century is characterised by phenomenal growth, one which materially eradicated traces of the landscape in which the city had been nurtured, in the inner city at least. As Sydney became denser and as buildings began to enclose the horizon, the vision of a city nestled amongst nature became increasingly blurred. The grid of streets laid down by Phillip, Macquarie and Mitchell became more sharply defined as technology both allowed for and demanded ever straighter routes for sewers, tram tracks, gas and, later, electricity and telephone lines. The port was transformed into a vast highway of shipping. The views of the harbour that had so delighted the early settlers were reserved for those wealthy enough to see it as an aquatic playground or indigent enough not to be tied into the activities of a city that looked inland, to the still substantially untapped resources of the continent.

The increase in the city's population and the introduction of trams and railways unlocked new areas for building. Industrial suburbs such as Balmain (ship building, timber and engineering), Newtown and St Peter's (tanning, brick making and wool washing) and Chippendale and Darlington (clothing and food processing) were established in the post-gold rush period. And in the late 1850s Paddington, Sydney's first commuter suburb, was formed out of the great estates on its eastern outskirts. The housing was usually terraced on the English model and constructed by small time speculative builders, leading one critic to observe: "We see hideous stretches of terraces and wildernesses of villas in painted brick and cement, decked up with meaningless ironwork and atrocious ornament."[35] Tram tracks were first laid in 1861 but ripped up five years later; they were unprofitable, reputedly noisy and the raised track proved a hindrance to conventional transport. They made a triumphant return in 1879 and, by 1884, 27.5 miles (44 kilometres) of track had been laid. Trams, pontificated the *Sydney Morning Herald* in 1882, enabled the working classes "to form homes in the healthier part of the suburbs, and afforded them ample opportunities of reaching, at moderate cost, the business and working centres of the city."[36] The first railway, connecting Sydney to Parramatta, opened in 1855 and over the next few decades was extended west and south. In the early 1890s, a line was constructed on the north side of the harbour. Notwithstanding the scope for real estate speculation, the driving rationale behind their construction was the transportation of freight; Sydney's wealth derived largely from its role as the principal port for the colony. During the 1860s and 1870s port activity moved gradually from Sydney Cove to the newly developed railway yard at Darling Harbour. It was already an industrial area. The first steam engine to operate in Australia, in 1813, was installed at Dickson's Mill. Other industries included P. N. Russell's engineering works (1842) and Thomas Sutcliffe Mort's New South Wales Fresh Food & Ice Company works (1861). From 1878 well into the early 1970s it was the principal port for the export of wool being ringed on its western side by an escarpment of gargantuan woolstores. In the adjacent district of Pyrmont, the Colonial Sugar Refinery Company established a vast plant for processing sugar cane in 1875.

Despite the incorporation of the city in 1842 and the creation of suburban municipalities in 1858, there was little or no control over the city's physical development, as the legislature was loath to devolve serious power or authority to local government. A contemporary report noted: "The plan adopted in the construction of cheap dwellings in Sydney is a very simple one. A wall is run up on the extreme back boundary of the allotment ... This is intersected by a number of partitions at right angles, at an average of 8 feet (2.4 metres) apart; a couple of cheap sashes for the upper and lower room, and one door on the ground floor for each house, and lo! the buildings when roofed are completed; and a property yielding good returns is created at minimum outlay."[37] In Sydney, as in the cities of Europe and North America, an increase in population led to a concomitant decline in the quality of the facilities afforded. One observer of the working class condition in Sydney, W. S. Jevons, was moved to remark that: "Nowhere have I seen such a retreat for filth and vice as the Rocks of Sydney. Few places could be found more healthily and delightfully situated but nowhere are the country and the beauty of nature so painfully contrasted with the misery and deformity which lie to the charge of man."[38] Despite the efforts of more socially conscious politicians and new health and sanitation authorities little was done to alleviate such miseries for nearly half a century. It took an outbreak of bubonic plague in 1900 for the problem to be addressed with any degree of thoroughness.

As the suburbs were an indicator of population growth, the city's expansion reflected its burgeoning wealth. In an attempt to assert its authority in the face of the colonial government's meddling in what it regarded as its affairs the city council embarked on a town hall of pompous proportions, designed in stages by various architects[39] between 1868 and 1889. Its tower loomed over the city skyline, along with that of another vital nineteenth-century institution, the General Post Office (1869-91) designed by the colonial architect James Barnet. In office between 1862 and 1890, Barnet produced a vast body of work. Aside from the General Post Office, he was responsible for extensions to the Australian Museum, the Colonial Secretary's Office (1869-75), the Lands Department (1876-94), the new Customs House (1887), the Sydney International Exhibition building (1878) and numerous hospitals, post offices, police stations and courthouses throughout Sydney. Barnet's architecture was conservative, his masonry ponderous and imbued with a sense of colonial gravitas but he revelled in his materials and accepted technological developments such as concrete, fire-resistant bricks and electricity. Whilst generally Italianate in appearance, his buildings eschew style in favour of monumental substance. Stylistic considerations though were still the meat and bread of public architecture. Writing in 1892 E. Wilson Dobbs, the assistant Victorian government architect, observed that over the last decade or so "a wave of more modern modes of architectural design is now being experienced through the colonies ... So Dutch-Queen Anne, French-Jacobean,

Garden Island seen from the Domain prior to it being razed, connected to Pott's Point and redeveloped as a naval base. Photographed by John Smith, about 1860.

Montagu Scott, *A day's picnic on Clarke Island, Sydney Harbour*, 1870.
The harbour is depicted as a playground for the well-clothed bourgeoisie of Sydney. Bathing was restricted by municipal regulations.

Lucien Henry's design for a public drinking fountain, about 1890. Its dome is based on the indigenous waratah flower.

Victorian-Elizabethan and Monumental-Queen Anne – not to mention Waterhouse-Normanesque and the Aston-Webb-cum-Collcutt style – jostle one another in our streets today."[40] And moving to Sydney in 1879, following his dismissal as Victorian government architect, William Wardell embarked on a series of stylistically diverse commissions, including the Flemish revival polychrome brickwork Australian Steam Navigation & Co building (1883-84) in The Rocks, the Renaissance revival New South Wales Club (1884-87) – a scaled-down version of Charles Barry's 1837 Reform Club in London – and St Mary's Cathedral (1865-99), an exercise in Puginesque Gothic. Thomas Rowe designed the Sydney Great Synagogue (1878) in an orientalist Italianate idiom and his competition winning Sydney Infirmary (now Sydney Hospital) was dished up in a mix of Italianate and French renaissance styles. This stylistic hodgepodge carried over into commercial buildings which, during the boom years of the 1880s, as property became increasingly valuable and new technologies – notably lifts – available, grew taller reaching ten or even twelve stories. Traditional architectural styles were ill-suited to such monsters; architects such as the John Sulman, Edward Raht and John Kirkpatrick designed impressive Beaux-Arts edifices in the American Romanesque idiom.[41] And imitating the preferences of banks and insurance companies, the City Council instructed its architect George McRae to design its new Queen Victoria Markets (1893-98) in a Byzantine version of the Romanesque style; he had offered them Gothic, Renaissance and Queen Anne alternatives.

The centenary of European settlement in Australia was marked in Sydney by the usual run of nineteenth-century festivities: " ... a feeble, fifth-rate drunk – a sort of combined scalp dance and gin conversazione ..."[42] the building of Centennial Hall to the designs of Thomas Sapsford and, significantly, the New South Wales premier Henry Parkes' inspired creation of Centennial Park amidst the sand dunes and bogs of the Lachlan Swamps near Paddington.[43] Not surprisingly, the focus of these celebrations was not the convict-tainted past but the future, a golden one of colonial federation, basking in the reflected glory and wealth of the British Empire. But the revelries were soon forgotten as the effect of the Argentine crisis of 1890 saw the flight of British capital from Australian banks, leading to their partial collapse and consequently a halt to most building works.

From the 1880s onwards a debate on what constituted a distinct national style simmered in the overheated offices of local architects. Prompted by the anticipated federation of the Australian colonies and a worldwide reaction to stylistic homogeneity and responding to issues such as climate, architects delved for an appropriate architectural form. In Sydney it was a suburban and domestic phenomenon, one largely based on the American Romanesque and shingle styles and the so-called Queen Anne revivals of Norman Shaw and his adherents. Early promoters of this "new" domestic architecture, such as John Horbury Hunt and Sulman, designed a number of grand detached villas in the developing semi-rural suburbs of the North Shore. In the late 1890s this synthetic style with its nationalistic undertones caught on, becoming increasingly popular, eventually passing into the repertoire of speculative builders and developers as the federation villa.[44] But attempts to extrapolate an architectural style from nationalist rhetoric were doomed in that there was no national myth to draw on – aside from that spurious one of convicts and their overseers –[45] and responses to the natural environment remained confused, best expressed in a series of illustrations by Lucien Henry, an École des Beaux-Arts-trained Frenchman.

Prepared for his unpublished book, *Australian Decorative Arts,* the plates depict unrealised buildings and objects derived awkwardly from the flora and fauna of New South Wales.[46] Henry's designs were more heraldry than architecture and whilst generally disregarded, the bias he reflected was embraced by suburban home dwellers in the decoration of their

Kirkham, near Narellan, John Horbury Hunt's grandiose villa (about 1885) on the outskirts of Sydney. Photographed about 1890.

otherwise Anglo-American houses. Paradoxically, it was this very focus on stylistic idiom that checked the emergence of a true regionalist architecture in Australia. For these early seekers after a sort of architectural truth, style was a paramount consideration in design. Little account was given to the wider context in which buildings were situated; it was either urban, suburban or rural and functional resolutions were often determined by the social status of occupants. Landscape and the environment – the two axioms of contemporary regionalist practice – were largely ignored by their predecessors for whom landscape was invariably reduced to a picturesque view and an environment was either healthy or unhealthy.

George Street in 1890, dominated by Barnet's General Post Office, Hilly's Commercial Banking Company building and Sulman's domed Bank of New South Wales (1889). Photograph by Charles Kerry.

George McRae's 1893 Queen Victoria Markets transformed into an office building. Photographed about 1920

Panorama of Sydney in 1888, after A. H. Fullwood.
Published in the centennial issue of the *Sydney Mail*.

The first stage of James Barnet's 1869 General Post Office.
Later extended and given a tower, it has recently been
converted into a hotel. Unknown photographer, about 1875.

William Wardell's St Mary's Cathedral designed in 1865
was substantially completed in 1928. Unknown
photographer, about 1900.

Stanton Rd Haberfield, 1911, as the epitome of suburbia, or the "real Australia." Photographed by Snape.

The New Century

On 1 January 1901 the six colonies of the Australian continent and Tasmania federated into one nation under the protection of the British

Federation and National Architecture

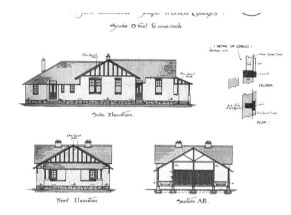

Crown. Thus Sydney emerged into the twentieth century with a population of 481,830 no longer the capital of the sovereign colony of New South Wales but one of six state capitals in the Commonwealth of Australia, governed – temporarily – from Melbourne. The political process of federation, along with the spoils generated by the providential discovery of gold at Kalgoorie in Western Australia, engendered a sense of economic and social optimism that, the First World War notwithstanding, would last until the economic depression of the 1930s when a collapse in commodity prices and another flight of British capital saw a third of the nation made unemployed.

The Aboriginals, displaced from their land, ghettoised at Kogarah, devastated by introduced diseases, were regarded as a dying race. Sydney was still essentially an Anglo-Irish society, the majority still deferring to Britain and its values. Only a minority faction sought to distance themselves from imperial allegiances. Their nationalistic hopes for an autonomous, independent Australia envisaged the creation of a united, democratic republic, populated by a race of sturdy white men and women, taking its place in the world, like America. But utopian dreams aside, official Sydney architecture at the beginning of the century remained quintessentially British, best encapsulated in the work of Barnet's successor as New South Wales government architect, Walter Liberty Vernon who held office between 1890 and 1911. His major public buildings reflect the architecture of empire: his Central Railway Station (1904-08), mounted over a colonnade of rusticated sandstone arches is topped by an asymmetrically placed Italianate clock tower; his designs for the National Gallery of New South Wales (1904-09) and the New South Wales Public Library (1905-10) with their ionic-columned porticoes are equally imperial in their conception.[47] Similarly, his Pyrmont and Darlinghurst Fire Stations (1907 and 1910), almost domestic in detailing with their sandstone-trimmed brickwork, appear almost like British Arts and Crafts houses of the previous century, their only obvious concession to local conditions being the use of the local Hawkesbury sandstone.

If the depression of the 1890s had frustrated the practice of a national architecture then the suburbs, "the real Australia",[48] provided a fertile ground for further exploration of

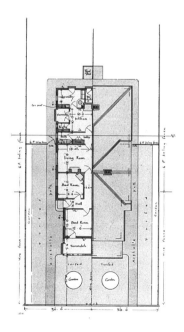

Plan, elevations and section of a house designed by W. H. Foggit for the New South Wales Housing Board's Dacey Garden Suburb (1913).

45

the dogma. The phenomenon of the Sydney suburb, with its vast tracts of land denuded of native vegetation, adumbrated into grids of red-tiled, brick-built, single-family houses of a notable sameness, has been viewed as the result of any number of factors including commercial speculation, the expansion of rail and tramways, the myth of Australian individualism – a desire to own one's own piece of land – and as a prophylactic against the possibilities of Bolshevik revolution.[49] In all probability, the Sydney suburbs resulted from an admixture of all these reasons linked to a burgeoning prosperity and effective propaganda campaigns initiated by the powerful combination of developers and the authorities. Life in the inner city districts was portrayed as unhealthy – if not fatal –, particularly after a 1900 outbreak of bubonic plague in The Rocks led to 103 deaths whereas life in the suburbs was life enhancing. Henry Gorman, a partner in the large and notoriously rapacious real estate agency Hardie & Gorman, declared: "In the suburbs subdivision follows subdivision, each latest one acting as pioneer for those that follow."[50] Improved public transport certainly made the suburbs possible but commercial speculation and development made them a reality.

Richard Stanton, a real estate agent and developer, was among the more successful speculators to build housing that catered to middle-class aspirations of acquiring a home of one's own. In 1902 he began subdividing into standard 150 by 50 foot (45.7 by 15.24 metre) blocks an 80 hectare site at Haberfield in western Sydney, promoting it as a model suburb: "Slum-less, lane-less and pub-less" where "all the residences are pretty, and nicely distanced from one another." The 1,500 houses "built to your order", were of the "federation" type: single-storey, detached, red-brick constructions with timber-framed verandahs surmounted by high-pitched roofs of slate or orange "Marseilles"-tiles, most being designed by Stanton's in-house architect J. Spencer-Stansfield. These "model villas" were surrounded by gardens that, if not strictly English in inspiration, were European in their planting; Australian flora was best appreciated as a decorative element in and on the house. It was a successful formula initiating a rash of imitations by other speculators, small builders, catalogue builders[51] and the state government, often aimed at those lower down the social spectrum, in suburbs such as Daceyville in 1912 (New South Wales Housing Board with planning based on the English "garden city" model by Sulman), Concord (1920) and Rosebery (1915). Stanton, the developer of Rosebery, used it as a testing ground for a new, cheaper style of house: an imported, prefabricated, Californian bungalow. While its timber construction proved inappropriate for local conditions, its form – adapted into standard brick – became fashionable immediately, not only with the average house builder but also with architects. By the early 1920s its low-gabled, wide-eaved roof had largely supplanted the federation villa in popular esteem.

The recurring debate on a national architecture continued to influence the design of houses in the more affluent eastern and North Shore suburbs. In 1912 the architect William Hardy Wilson began an intensive investigation into remaining examples of colonial architecture in a quest to discover appropriate forms. Twelve years later this obsession culminated in his self-published book *Old Colonial Architecture in New South Wales and Tasmania*. And just as the federation style had drawn on English and North American precedents so too did Hardy Wilson, who travelled through Europe and America between 1905 and 1909. His early houses, such as his own "Purulia" in Warrawee, a northern Sydney suburb (1914), reveal not only the inkling of an architectural language fusing classicism with the vernacular but an overt indebtedness to New England colonial revival styles.[52] Hardy Wilson's efforts to analyse and reveal the state's colonial architecture were (later) justifiably appreciated for their documentary value, but his endeavours to articulate an appropriate national form of architecture were ignored.

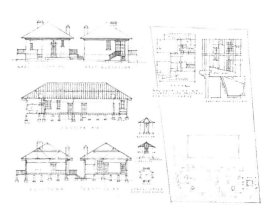

Plans, elevations and sections of "Purulia", the architect
W. Hardy Wilson's own house built in Fox Valley Road,
Warrawee, about 1914.

The Physics Building of the University of Sydney
designed in 1926 represented Leslie Wilkinson's Beaux-Arts
version of the Spanish mission style.

One of those contemporaries who appreciated Hardy Wilson's scholarship was Leslie
Wilkinson, appointed first professor of architecture at the University of Sydney in 1918.
Wilkinson, an Englishman, advocated the Californian Spanish Mission as a style suitable
for the better class house of Australians. His own home (1923), appropriately named
"Greenway" after Macquarie's civil architect, was an Australian colonial variant of the
Spanish Mission style, attested by Wilkinson as being most suited to the local climate.
And as architect to the university he was in a position to transfer the style out of the
domestic realm. His Physics Building (1926) successfully married Beaux-Arts structure to
Spanish Mission detailing. Wilkinson was not responsible for designing the apotheosis of
the style that he had so promoted. "Boomerang", an opulent mansion in Elizabeth Bay,
was designed in 1926 by the cosmopolitan Englishman Neville Hampson; of all the Spanish
Mission buildings in Sydney, it was closest to the ersatz Californian origins of the style.[53]
Both the Colonial Revival and Spanish Mission styles were later grafted onto the basic
suburban bungalow type as an alternative to stockbroker Tudor, Californian bungalow
and decorative modern styles.

But the most radical and innovative approach to the Sydney suburban landscape came
not from Australia but from America. It had little to do either with the appropriateness of
styles or local debates concerning a national architecture; its promoters were largely
marginalised by the great and good who knew best. Walter Burley Griffin and his wife

47

Castlecrag, the denuded landscape and the houses built by the architects Walter Burley Griffin and his wife Marion Mahony, probably photographed by Griffin, about 1924.

Marion Mahony Griffin, both former employees of Frank Lloyd Wright, arrived in Sydney from Chicago. Griffin had won the controversial competition to plan a new federal capital in 1912. To an enraptured audience of local worthies Griffin reputedly proclaimed that Sydney "was five times more beautiful than he had ever dreamt ... Sydney should be the most beautiful garden city the world has ever seen ..."[54] He then departed for Melbourne to work on his project for Canberra. Stymied in his attempts to design the city by a combination of political chicanery, bureaucratic interference and public indifference the architect resigned from his post as Federal Capital Director of Design and Construction in 1919 and opened an office in Sydney. In 1920 Griffin and Mahony established the Greater Sydney Development Association Limited and acquired a 259 hectare site at Castlecrag. Their approach to its development flew in the face of received ideas as to how such a project should progress: rather than obliterating the existing landscape — the norm for Sydney suburban developments — they preserved and nurtured what was there. In place of a grid of geometrical precision they extended roads that responded to the topography and natural features of the site. Instead of converting the whole area into private lots they interspersed it with communal reserves aimed at creating a sense of community, insisting that the buildings erected be subordinate to the landscape. Their architecture was no less radical, its form derived from those same ideas that underlay the Griffins' approach to the landscape. Built of massive sandstone masonry, Griffin's patented Knit-lock system and concrete with, wherever possible, flat roofs, their houses were distinctive and, by Sydney standards, radically advanced. The depression along with the remoteness of the suburb — the Harbour Bridge only opened in 1932 — spelt the end of the Griffins' dream, and they designed only thirty-five of the suburb's houses. But whilst not completed to the Griffins' designs Castlecrag was a thriving development, fulfilling the uncommercial aims of integrating suburban development into the landscape and creating a distinctive residential community. Notwithstanding the Prairie School refe-

rences in their houses, the Griffins succeeded in creating an architectural system based on principles drawn not only from nature – the landscape – but also from an idealised vision of future life – the community –, a distinct local style of both architecture and subdivision. Yet in spite of the praise lavished on it, the Castlecrag scheme had little immediate influence on future suburban development in Sydney.

The terror of epidemics such as bubonic plague, smallpox and tuberculosis not only popularised suburban lifestyles but also spurred an appreciation of the benefits of town planning in Sydney. An obsession of Sulman's – he was elected first president of the Town Planning Association of New South Wales in 1913 – planning was again the subject of acrimonious political debate during the first decade of the century as the city council and the state government indulged in one of their periodical wrangles over who should control the city's development. Slums and their clearance were one of the more contentious issues in this petulant debate. They were perceived as the breeding ground of disease, poverty, and vice, and the council was keen to see them removed from within the city's precincts; they were damaging to business and the land could be more profitably developed for commercial and industrial purposes. Sulman's agitation stirred the state government into setting up a Commission for the Improvement of Sydney in 1907. Its report resulted in new legislation in 1912 – largely based on the British 1909 *Town Planning Act* – which enabled cosmetic changes to be made to the city's street pattern.

Imperial splendour: Walter Liberty Vernon's Central Railway Station completed in 1908. Unknown photographer, 1923.

As well, the council was given the power to resume and demolish slums and, uniquely for New South Wales, undertake municipal housing schemes. It was a power not exercised with great enthusiasm. Slums were cleared in vast swathes but they were replaced by factories, shops and offices, not houses. Displaced inner city residents were encouraged to join the stampede to the suburbs. A handful of municipal housing schemes were planned, notably Robert Broderick's proto-modernist Strickland Buildings in Chippendale (1912-14)[55] and Way's Terrace Worker's Housing in Pyrmont (1923-26).[56] The latter scheme was designed by Wilkinson, along with Joseph Fowell, in his Spanish Mission style and equipped with all manners of modern conveniences such as private bathrooms and lavatories, but despite the amenities they were not popular.[57]

In contrast to the suburbs, the inner city had little interest in the national architecture debate. Sydney enterprises still wanted buildings imitating those of London and New York. The first two decades of the century saw the Beaux-Arts style continue to exert its influence on commercial and public architecture. The size of these buildings was limited to 150 feet (45.7 metres) by the *Height of Buildings Act* introduced in 1912 as a result of public outcry at the 170 foot (51.8 metres) height of Culwulla Chambers designed by one of the more prolific practices Spain & Cosh in 1911-12. More utilitarian in character than

The Duke of York (later George V) advancing down William Street during Federation celebrations in April 1901. Unknown photographer.

previous commercial buildings – such as those designed around the turn of the century by Sulman, Kirkpatrick and Raht – Culwulla Chambers heralded the arrival of the commercial *palazzo* style, one which until comparatively recently overshadowed the streets of the central business district. It was a style particularly favoured by banks and insurance companies. In 1923 the Commercial Banking Company of Sydney commissioned Kent & Massie to design its headquarters in George Street, at the foot of Martin Place. Four years later the Bank of New South Wales rebuilt its headquarters on the adjoining site; designed by Robertson & Marks its façade politely matched that of its neighbour but a vast arched portico was substituted in lieu of the former's colonnade. The difference was in the detail, not in the substance.

"Barncleuth", architect George Sydney Jones's own house (about 1910) in Pennant Hills.

Quite extraordinarily, the national style debate prompted a wave of radical architecture that, in some respects, parallels early developments of Modernism overseas. Its proponents advocated flat roofs and a reduction of detail, stressed functional considerations and alluded to so-called vernacular features such as verandahs. But its nationalistic focus overwhelmed the embryonic functionalism it had briefly encouraged. It was more important to design for Australians than to adhere to theoretical positions that focussed on the fitness of the building or the object to fulfil its purpose. The significance of this functionalist experiment was recognised by a minority; its star petered out amidst a slough of indifference as its partisans reverted to conventional architectural solutions. Not surprisingly, the two schools of architecture in the city – at the University of Sydney and the Sydney Technical College – remained enthralled with the decorative flourishes and stepped orders of the Beaux-Arts well into the 1930s. And even if students of these two schools were drawn to more challenging architectural forms, the realities were such that they could never build them.[58]

Notable amongst those working in a functionalist idiom was George Sydney Jones who, in the first decade of the century, designed houses which broke with convention in having flat roofs and corridor-less planning.[59] He argued that Australian architects should make use of contemporary technology and new ideas to produce an architecture that was "a true reflex of the age in which we live",[60] rejecting the revivalism proposed as appropriate architectural idioms for the continent by Sulman, Hardy Wilson and Wilkinson. Jones's most notable houses, "Barncleuth" in Pennant Hills (his own house), "Lorne" (now known as "Rochester") in Beecroft and "Luleo" in Strathfield were built between 1909 and 1911. In their outward form they resembled the work of more audacious British and American architects such as Edwin Lutyens and Charles Voysey as well as that of the Vienna Secession such as Otto Wagner and Joseph Olbrich. As with so many of his professional colleagues, Jones's acquaintance with the work of these proto-Modernists was derived from publications but in his youth he had travelled in the Mediterranean and his observation of the flat-roofed vernacular buildings he encountered influenced directly his efforts to address the perennial issue of climate in local architecture. Jones's proselytising fell for the most part onto barren ground, as few architects were prepared to risk cuboid forms, deep verandahs and flat roofs in a small, essentially conservative, society. Sydney architecture of the pre-First World War period remained deeply entrenched in the ditch of revivalism.

The First World War exposed a whole generation to overseas developments in architecture as well as catalysing the establishment – in 1915 – of the first steel mill in Australia at Newcastle, allowing steel-framed buildings to be a more realistic proposition.[61] Only in the postwar period were modern technologies widely used in the construction of buildings. These "advanced methods of construction" were evoked in efforts to justify the Modernism of design. But Modernism was not just a matter of new technology, it was a fundamentally different approach to the way buildings were designed, encompassing issues of function and form, advocating a new role for architecture within a primarily urban landscape. In Sydney it was considered and criticised merely as a new style: an anonymous Sydney architect in 1930 declared that Le Corbusier's architecture "outrages the normal intelligence ... lacks harmony, rhythm and general design"[62] whilst another ascribed its development to "a small coterie of enthusiasts [who] banded together in Paris with the

BMA House, Macquarie Street, designed by Fowell & McConnell in 1928. Note the giant sculptural koalas on the façade. Unknown photographer, about 1934.

object of introducing a new architecture ... shorn of all superfluous ornament and expressed in its true structural form."[63] Those postwar buildings erected in Sydney employing new technologies were neither modern in their appearance – in the sense of being "abstract" – nor modern in their organisation – in the sense of their appearance reflecting their structure and function. Historically – no matter how stylistically conservative they were – Sydney architects had shown general interest in making use of innovative technologies. Steel frames, reinforced concrete and architectural terracotta panels were used in the construction of such innately conventional buildings as the British Medical Association House in Macquarie Street designed by Joseph Fowell and Kenneth McConnell in 1928. It won a Royal Institute of British Architects bronze medal in 1934, an award originating in Britain set up "to encourage fine examples of street architecture and to recognise buildings which have been significant in developing the public taste."[64] Whilst superficially different from the commercial *palazzi* erected in the inner city, its pastiche quasi-Gothic façade – complete with sculptural koalas – and a fumed oak-panelled lobby reveal it to have more in common with them than the buildings of international Modernism. Wilkinson, as chairman of the local jury, declared that the BMA building was "the first in Sydney to throw emphasis on general mass rather than concentrate on the effect of the front elevation."[65] Modernism was perceived not only by the public but also by many architects as a manifestation of box-type buildings with glass façades. For most, including Wilkinson, it was merely a form of surface decoration best conveyed through the formal syntax of the Beaux-Arts.

The spectacular volumes and Mayan motifs
of Walter Burley Griffin's 1934 Pyrmont incinerator.
Photographed by Max Dupain in 1965.

The polemic between the promoters of traditionalism and the adherents of abstraction was encapsulated in the debates surrounding the design of the Sydney Harbour Bridge. This icon of modern structural technology was dressed in the trappings of a monument. Its granite-faced pylons play no structural role but were added to censor the impact of raw technology for a visually conservative public. The idea of a bridge linking the city with its northern suburbs had been a political football since the 1880s. It became a reality in 1922 when the New South Wales government, acting under the guidance of its director of public works J. J. C. Bradfield, passed an enabling bill committing itself to construction. Designed primarily by the British engineer Ralph Freeman, its impact on the city's infrastructure was considerable. Not only were innumerable buildings demolished to make way for the bridge approaches but, from henceforth, the car constituted an essential element of the streetscape. In 1921 there were 28,665 registered motor vehicles in New South Wales, by 1939 this figure had exploded to 327,628. And the North Shore increasingly became the favoured haunt of commuters as the bridge carried 100,000 of them in and out of the city, daily. Under construction throughout the economic depression of the early 1930s the Sydney Harbour Bridge became symbolic of the city's hopes and aspirations; it was painted, photographed and engraved from every angle both during and after its construction. Its inauguration in 1932 by the Labor premier, John Lang, attracted considerable political controversy. It was thought by many of those who were to use it that the opening should have been performed by, if not the British king himself, then by one of his representatives in Australia.

C. Bruce Dellit, *ANZAC War Memorial, Hyde Park,*
1930. A watercolour of this 1929
competition-winning scheme.

Harold Cazneaux, *West Circular Quay*, 1931, showing Macquarie's soon-to-be-demolished Commissariat (1815) and-nearing completion-the Sydney Harbour Bridge.

Walter Burley Griffin was a voice crying out in this wilderness of conformity. He received no public commissions. However, from the late 1920s, he designed a series of incinerators for the Reverbatory Incinerator and Engineering Company which were remarkable not only for their advanced technology and their sophisticated design but for the fact that Griffin transformed industrial buildings into essential components of the landscape. He attested that "the final test of Modernism is the replacement of industrial eyesores with public amenities ... It has been intended [for] these buildings also to awaken an aversion to the fundamentally uneconomic conditions of industrial ugliness."[66] Located primarily in the suburbs – there were eight in Sydney – Griffin's best-known incinerator was erected at Pyrmont in 1934 on a high site overlooking Blackwattle Bay. It was a breathtaking exercise in articulated massing: a high sandstone wall acting as a pediment supported a low horizontal block, faced with concrete panels stamped with a pattern of fluid "Mayan" motifs, all surmounted by a rectangular-sectioned smoke stack. Shortly after its completion, disheartened by his Australian experiences, Griffin left the country for India in 1935 where he died two years later. Griffin's Modernism was ignored, by and large, and his language of forms misunderstood even by architects keen to jump onto the bandwagon of modern architecture. His approach to the landscape, as exemplified in his schemes for Castlecrag and the incinerators, is still largely perceived in terms of the buildings, not in terms of the context. As recently as 1992 his Pyrmont incinerator, one of the two buildings he designed in the city, was demolished to muted protest; the other, the Tatler and Australian Picture Palace, was destroyed in the early 1980s.[67]

A Melbourne commentator noted archly that "Sydney architecture isn't a conscious development on something that has gone before – it is simply a following of a fashion. Architects have not consciously designed their buildings because they like the look of them, but because every other country is designing buildings like them."[68] In Sydney a branch of Modernism that was international in inspiration and notably different from that of the local school emerged in the late 1930s that was more than just a stylistic consideration, it was a new way of building. Young Sydney architects seduced by a repertoire of flat planes and reductive forms found first-hand inspiration overseas – usually "home" to London – or, secondhand, from those fortunate enough to have travelled, as well as from international and the few local publications. Returnees included Arthur Stephenson, Arthur Baldwinson and Sydney Ancher who would all become prominent interpreters of the International Style in the ensuing years. Stephenson had studied in both Melbourne and Sydney before serving as a soldier in the First World War. Following this he studied at the Architectural Association in London before returning to establish what became the largest architectural practice in Australasia. Baldwinson who had worked for the Australian-born Raymond McGrath, Maxwell Fry and Walter Gropius in London returned to be employed by the older Stephenson before himself launching into private practice. From 1936 on, Stephenson Meldrum & Turner built a string of impressive Modernist public and commercial buildings, notably AGM (later ACI)[69] House. Sydney Ancher won a travelling scholarship in 1930 remaining in Europe until 1935 where he was exposed to the work of international Modernists such as Mies Van der Rohe, Le Corbusier and Wilhelm Marinus Dudok as well as that of the English Modernists. On his return to Sydney he worked briefly for Emil Sodersten before entering into a partnership with his former employer, the relatively conservative Reginald Prevost whose house he designed in 1936.[70] With its curved volumes and glass brick walls it was a villa type of house that could well have featured in F. R. S. Yorke's influential 1934 publication *The Modern House*.[71]

But in Sydney the Decorative Modernism – now often described as Art Deco – of the generally untravelled local school held sway. Its pantheon was C. Bruce Dellit's 1929

Map of Sydney Harbour and Surrounding Districts, published by the North South Wales Department of Lands in 1915.

Emil Sodersten's 1934 Decorative Modernist City Mutual insurance building, photographed soon after completion.

competition-winning design for the ANZAC (Australian and New Zealand Army Corps) War Memorial in Hyde Park, a sentimental exercise in monumental massing. Dellit's work – hailed locally as a forerunner of Modernism –[72] was matched by that of Sodersten who, in 1926, won the competition for the Canberra War Memorial (completed in 1941). Sodersten's work ranged from office buildings to hotels, notably his City Mutual insurance building (1934) and the prestigious Hotel Australia (1936).[73] Decorative Modernism was essentially a marketing exercise which evoked the "modernity" of Hollywood and provided a client with an up-to-date image of efficiency without confronting the issues explored by the more rigorous international style. In the redevelopment of Elizabeth Bay the values associated with Decorative Modernism were deployed as a marketing tool to justify an increase in urban density. From 1925 this former "genteel suburb" underwent a dramatic transformation as apartment buildings rose out of the gardens and grottoes of colonial villas. It was promoted as the antithesis of suburbia, whilst simultaneously responding to suburban concerns about the evils of inner city living. "By enabling reasonable concentration, the flat has aided considerably in slum clearance by enabling the best to be made from a confined rebuilding area ... Flats cannot be vicious of themselves. Well built and properly supervised they are a modern development of great value, destined to play a part in the forward march of the human race",[74] declared the *Constructional Review*.

Moreover Modernism was seen as an appropriate style for flats because it "led to sunshine and light and healthier living."[75] Sodersten's Birtley Towers (1934) in Elizabeth Bay drew on American prototypes for its organisation and its brickwork is reminiscent of a favourite source for Sydney Modernists, Dudok's Hilversum town hall. And far from addressing the issues implicit in slum clearance the Elizabeth Bay apartment buildings were marketed

61

Civic Hotel designed by Sydney Ancher for Tooth & Co. Photographed by Sam Hood in 1941, shortly after completion.

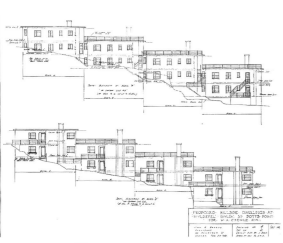

as being appropriate for "business couples or a woman with outside interests such as the avid golfer or bridge player."[76] Decorative Modernism was also adopted as a house style by the Sydney brewers Tooth & Co for their extensive chain of pubs in the mid 1930s. Existing premises were stripped of their polished wood and brass interiors and given new, beigy-yellow tile[77] and chromed metal fit-outs. New buildings were dressed with façades of curved brick walls, continuous glazing and cantilevered awnings. And while the style reflected an image of modernity it was also supremely practical. The glazed interiors could be hosed down by publicans after the ruckus of the "six o'clock swill", as drinking in public was illegal after 6:00 p.m.

In 1938 Sydney was the venue for the British Empire Games, the first such occasion for demonstrating the city's obsession with hosting sporting events but, unlike later sporting extravaganzas, little new was built for the games. By September 1939 when Australia, following in the footsteps of Britain, declared war on Germany Sydney's Modernist variants had won an undeclared battle of the styles, in the city at least. And in its own idiosyncratic way Sydney had developed an architectural form and an urban structure that was quite singular. Admittedly it was provincial, derivative and dated by comparison with international prototypes, it arose in a climate largely devoid of theoretical considera-tion, and it was designed for the greater part by architects or builders subject to the whims of clients more interested in financial advantage than concern with design.

Luxury Modernism in an inner city district: John Brogan
& Associates' Wyldefel Gardens in Elizabeth Bay.
Contemporary photographs and 1935 plans.

Sydney Ancher's 1936 Prevost House in Bellevue Hill designed soon after his return from Europe.

Aerial views of Sydney photographed by John Park, about 1931.
The building of the approaches to the Harbour Bridge cut swathes through large sections of the existing residential fabric of both The Rocks and North Sydney.

Following pages:

Bondi Beach, Sydney, or the beginnings of the cult of the body and life on the beach. John Park, about 1935.

After the Second World War

The decades that followed the Second World War saw a major shift in Australia's international loyalties. This had been anticipated in 1942 by the Commonwealth prime minister, the Labor Party's John Curtin, who declared soon after the start of the Pacific war: "I make it quite clear that Australia looks to America free of any pangs as to our traditional links or kinship with the United Kingdom."[78] Britain was no longer the source of received political or social wisdoms. And although Britons still comprised the greater part of the country's migrant intake they were now joined by Dutch, Germans, Yugoslavs, Greeks and Italians, the latter mostly from the south. But the country in which these "new Australians" arrived was far from the earthly paradise evoked in the government's migrant propaganda. Until the Korean War revived trade the country lay in the grips of economic depression. In Sydney there was a shortage not only of housing but also of the materials and skilled workmen with which to build them. Returned servicemen and young families moved into the parental home, verandahs were enclosed with fibro-cement sheeting and glass-louvred blinds to become bedrooms.

Migrations

Sydney in 1956. Bennelong Point in the foreground is occupied by a tramshed.

These were the decades which saw life in the suburbs entrenched firmly as "the Australian way of life." As the country grew more prosperous so too consumer demand for the trappings of suburban life became increasingly evident. The Melbourne-based *Meanjin* – one of the few intellectual journals available at the time – published a particularly scathing attack on this ideal: "Behold the Man – the Australian man of today – on Sunday mornings in the suburbs, when the high decibel drone of the motor-mower is calling the faithful to worship. A block of land, a brick veneer, and the motor-mower beside him in the wilderness – what more does he want to sustain him except a Holden to polish, a beer with the boys, marital sex on Saturday night, a few furtive adulteries, an occasional gamble on the horses or the lottery, the tribal rituals of football, the flickering shadows in his lounge room of cops and robbers, goodies and baddies, guys and dolls?"[79] In 1948, reflecting these suburban ambitions the state government published its first masterplan for the County of Cumberland, in effect for the greater Sydney region. This scheme epitomised garden city planning, proposing amongst other measures, a green belt which would girdle the city from the north (Ku-ring-gai National Park) through to the south (Royal National Park). Sydney, with a population of 1,700,000 was expanding rapidly. The demand for housing was considerable yet architects had little or no role to play in most

Moored on Bennelong Point, the sculptural form of the Sydney Opera House has become a symbol of both the city and the country.

The Rose Seidler house at Turramurra (1948) is a fine example
of the importation of the International Style by expatriate European
architects. Designed by Harry Seidler shortly after his arrival in Sydney.

The plan of the Rose Seidler house was inspired
by Marcel Breuer with whom Seidler worked
in the USA.

of the houses erected. Many were constructed on a self-build basis, even services such as plumbing, sewerage and wiring were installed by amateurs, and the necessary permits would be acquired by paying tradesmen illegally to certify that the work conformed with the regulations. Architects were increasingly employed on projects further away from the city centre, particularly to the north of the city, where the population tended to be wealthier. The period was to see the consolidation of Modernism and the start of a reaction leading to an increasingly organic domestic architecture, one more attuned with the environment.

An immediate consequence of the war was a change in the diffusion of Modernist approaches to architecture in Australia, largely brought about by the arrival of European architects fleeing the clutches, and the aftermath, of Nazism. The phenomenon began at the end of the 1930s with the arrival in Sydney of the Germans Hugh and Eva Buhrich, ending in the late 1940s with the immigration of the architect who would become Australia's best-known Modernist, Harry Seidler. The expatriates who brought and practiced the principles of European Modernism in Australia also experienced the advantages to be gained in confronting geographical conditions unknown in Europe. This is especially true in the case of Hugh Buhrich whose diverse architectural education inclined him more toward experimentation than the pursuit of architectural dogmas. Born in Hamburg in 1911, Buhrich first thought of becoming an engineer, but it was architecture that he eventually studied in Berlin, under Hans Poelzig, after which he worked for Alfred Roth in Zurich. Arriving in England in 1938 he migrated soon after to Sydney, building a house for

Interior and exterior views of the architect Harry Seidler's own house at Killara, 1957.

Flat roof, open plan and a verandah are the main features of Sydney Ancher's own house at Neutral Bay, 1957

himself at Castlecrag in 1941. He practiced architecture discreetly, hindered by the refusal of the Royal Australian Institute of Architects to recognise his qualifications. Nonetheless he was one of the unseen heroes of the local scene and the designer of a number of remarkable schemes, many of them now sadly mutilated to the point of destruction by unsympathetic modifications: a number of small office blocks, two synagogues and numerous houses. Wherever he built he demonstrated an exceptional capacity for adapting his design to suit the site, the function and his client as well as exhibiting a taste for structural challenges that resulted in spectacular plastic expression. His own house in Castlecrag – the second – which he built himself in 1972, an extension to an existing Griffin Knitlock house, is a structural and spatial tour de force responding both to the precipitous topography of the site and to the landscape of Middle Harbour. The house is anchored to the slope by a double cantilever structure while its internal volume marries an open plan, marked by subtle changes in floor level, to a near-Baroque virtuosity in the modelling of the spaces.

In 1948 Harry Seidler arrived in this new New World. In contrast to Buhrich's modesty, Seidler is an architect whose work has had considerable impact on the city: for its scope, given that he has built in most parts of Sydney; for its diversity, both in the inner city and in numerous, quite disparate suburbs; for the durability and notoriety of a career that has spanned five decades and which has resulted in several international publications of note;[80] for the influential role he has played in the city's culture. Born in Vienna in 1923, he left for England in 1938, then was forcibly removed (as an enemy alien) to Canada. He subsequently studied architecture at the Harvard University Graduate School of Design where he was taught by two of the former Bauhaus masters, Marcel Breuer and Walter Gropius.

The Arrow Motor's showroom in Double Bay by Arthur Baldwinson, 1956. The Holden is the Australian "national" car.

The house of architect Bruce Rickard in Warrawee,
1959. Interconnected spaces and natural materials inspired by
the architecture of Frank Lloyd Wright.

An opportunity to work with Oscar Niemeyer saw him move to Brazil before migrating to Sydney to rejoin his family who had preceded him. Seidler is undoubtedly the only architect of his generation who, wherever he has built, has pursued and defended the ideas expressed by the founders of European Modernism, in particular those of Gropius and Le Corbusier. For Seidler, Sydney has been a place of opportunity as well as a context relatively devoid of the radical ideas and forms that had nourished his architecture, an ideal platform from which to launch a crusade for a "new architecture."

Seidler designed his first house in 1948 for his parents – the Rose Seidler House – in an outlying suburb north of Sydney. Soon after it was completed it featured in a number of international architectural publications. Whereas local colleagues such as Ancher, Bald-winson and Douglas Snelling sought to interpret – sometimes ponderously – the models of the International Style, the Rose Seidler house is archetypal Breuer. With its square plan, its concrete assertiveness and through its use of materials, it sits with aplomb on a surface stripped of its natural vegetation, clearly articulating an architectural manifesto. From one house to another and from one court case to the next (the building permits he submitted invariably aroused the fury of conservative local councils and his houses were the subject of polemical resistance in the local press), Seidler swiftly imposed his personality, his aesthetic and his vision of the architect's role on a largely provincial society, unwilling to confront change. His militancy drove him to propose urban schemes directly influenced by the tenets of the Athens Charter. One example is his masterplan for McMahon's Point, on the north shore of the harbour: only Blue's Point Tower, at the tip of the headland, was built and it still arouses controversy.

In the mid 1950s the architecture of the individual house was revealing a new orientation. Seeking a close rapport between daily life and the native landscape these houses were tied to the topography of sites through divided levels, complex plans and sloping roofs; trees were retained to play a natural role of filtering and providing shade from the sun. The buil-

Regional Romanticism

dings demonstrated a new accord with the landscape, thanks to the use of simple – often untreated – local materials. This new consideration for the environment responded, in part, to particular conditions resulting from the economic situation in Sydney. The endemic lack of qualified tradesmen and materials prompted the use of whatever was readily available for economical buildings: roughly sawn timber, clinker brick and concrete tiles. A strong demand for housing encouraged the subdivision of land remote from the centre, particularly to the north west, where architects were confronted by barely serviced sites, clumps of vegetation and slopes strewn with sandstone outcrops, forming a characteristic landscape, evoking a nature of origin.

This architectural tendency, akin to a sort of regional romanticism, has been dubbed "Sydney School" notwithstanding the disparity of allegiances grouped under this appellation. It developed in reaction to the rationalism and abstraction of the International Style that dominated experimental architecture and was particularly associated with Melbourne. Nevertheless "Sydney School" architects did not dissociate themselves from the debates coursing through the Modern Movement in Europe initiated by young architects contesting the dogmas of the founding fathers.[81] Following the example of the British, the references of architects diversified. They now looked to those parts of the world where the Modernist vocabulary had adapted to a local way of life in an osmosis with

A shack in a tree: the Lucas house at Castlecrag designed by Bill and Ruth Lucas in 1957.

nature. Their journeys to Europe henceforth focused on Scandinavia, notably Finland. And apart from a renewal of attention in the work of Frank Lloyd Wright there developed a new interest in California where the climate and the maritime landscape resembles that of coastal Sydney. Californian journals, notably *Architecture & Arts*, disseminated the work of Rudolf Schindler, Richard Neutra and Gordon Drake, the latter being accorded added respect for his Japanese influences. On the other side of the Pacific Peter Muller from 1953 and Bruce Rickard from 1957 sought to acclimatise Wright's organic principles: dynamic open plans, generated by the articulation of wings around a nucleus of services; deft interpenetrations of interiors and exteriors; a marked preference for natural timber and stone. The layout (in section) and the materials used by Ken Woolley for his own house in Mosman (1962) reveal the architect's interest in the work of Alvar Aalto. The Jacobs House in Wahroonga (1963) with its post and beam structure and its elongated planes of brick wall demonstrates the influence of the Japanese tradition on its architect Russell Jack. Bill Lucas defended an extremist position sustained by a belief that the best architecture is no architecture at all. With his wife Ruth he built in 1957 an exemplary shack-like home out of rough-sawn timber, fibro-cement sheeting and glass-louvred windows, those same materials used in more conventional suburban houses. Perched in the bush, it encapsulates in a single structure the spirit of the times. These rough-built houses transformed what had been a constraint into an ideal; the difficult sites on which the "Sydney School" had been forced to build became increasingly sought after. It was a tendency that redefined the relationship between the architecture of the house and the city's unique landscape, an idea that has matured into the dominant lightweight and open architecture of the city today.

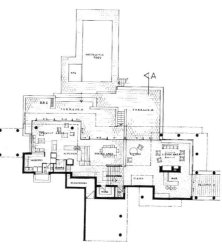

Bruce Rickard's Curry house at Bayview.

Architect Ken Woolley's own house at Mosman (1962) is a response to the constraints and advantages of a site.

The Opera House. Photographed by Max Dupain 1973.

Incontestably the most significant architectural event of the 1960s was the construction of the Sydney Opera House. Given to the city by the Australian Labor Party state government

The Opera House

A site meeting in 1964 between Jørn Utzon (left) and Norman Ryan, the North South Wales Labor Minister for Public Works.

the previous decade, the building provided Sydney with the lasting international reputation it had long been seeking. By its very nature, its scale and its ambitious programme the enterprise was sparkling testimony to the optimism that animated the authorities in the years of prosperity that followed the Korean War. It reflected the will of a still provincial society as it clambered up to a position amongst the great capitals of the world. The idea of building a great multi-functional cultural centre in the city, one able to be used for concerts and conferences, had been circulating in the world of officialdom for some years. In 1955, following an impulsive decision by the New South Wales premier John Joseph Cahill, the idea became a reality. The following year the state government announced an open international competition, worldwide one of the first of the post war period. From the outset of what would become a true adventure everything was unusual for Sydney: the competition was international and not national as had been advocated briefly. And it was to be judged by a quartet of architects, two locals and two eminent ones from overseas: the Englishman Leslie Martin, the principal designer of the Royal Festival Hall in London, built five years previously, and the Finnish-American Eero Saarinen who had just started work on the shells of his TWA Terminal at Idlewild (now J. F. Kennedy) Airport in New York. Furthermore, the site selected – Bennelong Point, the finger of land that terminates Circular Quay East, extending down from the Botanic Gardens – was equally unexpected, even if today it seems that there could have been no other. The new Opera House replaced a tramshed built following the demolition of Fort Macquarie around the turn of the century. Far from being the tourist and recreational facility it is today, the harbour in 1956 was still a working port, a location for commerce, industry and naval activities, particularly to the west of the Harbour Bridge. The wharves at Dawes Point, and further to the west, at Walsh Bay, Pyrmont and Darling Harbour were ringed by vast warehouses and factories, trafficking in the products that gave the nation its wealth: coal, wheat, minerals, wool and sugar. Overlooking a harbour crossed by ferries and steamships, separated from the fabric of the city, Bennelong Point at first appeared to be an improbable location for so prestigious a building. Nevertheless, on the recommendation of a committee of experts assembled to advise the government as to the location of the building and in the face of competing options, this harbour site was eventually selected for its strategic position on what was the natural focus of the city. The programme devised for the building, was simplicity itself and its openness proof of a refreshing candour. It required the provision of two halls, a great multi-functional auditorium and a smaller hall for chamber music along with ancillary facilities – foyers, rehearsal rooms, balconies and restaurants. The competition was distinguished, finally, by its respect for the rules of procedure, in particular for the anonymity of the candidates, by the absence of a preconceived aesthetic on the part of the client, two reasons underlying the jury's audacious choice, and by the fact that the consequence of the jury's decision would be supported by the government for as long as it remained in power.

The Opera House saga proper began on 27 January 1957 when a largely unknown thirty eight-year old Danish architect, Jørn Utzon, was declared the winner of a competition that had attracted over two hundred submissions from around the world. The jurors, Eero Saarinen in particular, had been seduced by the image of a fan of white shells that Utzon proposed opening over the face of this maritime landscape, sheltering the two auditoria. A monumental staircase descended at the southern end of a massive platform on which

the shells rested, capturing views from the Botanic Gardens. It was an image of enduring strength, one admirably suited to the site, declared a jury seduced by the fitness and originality of the project. Utzon explained his desire to give the city a fresh face through his new civic building. He declared that he had been inspired by the clouds and geology of the harbour, evoking ancient pre-Columbian and Chinese temples to justify his vast platform and the stepped levels of his staircase. The ideas embodied in his project expressed the ideals that European Modernism espoused in the 1950s: a reappraisal of the lessons of history, an interest in traditional urban forms and the reclaiming of greater formal and sculptural freedom made possible by the appearance of new technologies, in particular thin shells of reinforced concrete.

Thus Sydney became a city invested with the most advanced, the most radical and, unquestionably the most poetic project of the time, one that embodied all of what Sigfried Giedion would label as characteristic of "the third generation of Modernism."[82] It was a privilege not without its inconveniences. Experimental in all respects, the building arose slowly through fifteen years of arduous work, between marvelling attention on the one hand, and sometimes violent criticism on the other. Utzon won the competition through the convincing power of a lyrical image. He then had to resolve the problems of such a

Bennelong Point became an artificial platform out of which arose the curved concrete roofs, assembled piece by piece like a meccano set.

project as the construction progressed. The erection of the monumental plinth was the first stage of work to be undertaken. Within three years Bennelong Point had been transformed into a sort of artificial geology, containing all the necessary facilities onto which the two seating tiers of the hall were carved like a sculpture. Then the three fanning unfurled "sails" were raised on the platform. Initially conceived of as thin concrete shells – a solution abandoned after four years of fruitless calculation by the structural engineers, the London-based Ove Arup & Partners – they were finally realised in the manner of Gothic vaults through an assemblage of concrete segments prefabricated on the site, rather like a giant Meccano set. The geometry of their convex surfaces, which at last permitted the realisation of their forms, is generated by the dimensions of the same virtual sphere; these were then clad in panels set with a pattern of glossy and mat white tiles, also prefabricated on the site. Finally, as Utzon was resolving the design of the last stage of work – the glazed façades of the shell openings, the interiors and the auditoria along with internal and external finishes – he clashed with a newly elected conservative state government. He was driven to leave the job in early 1966. It was completed, after a fashion, by three Australian architects.[83] In a sort of irony, Utzon's mutilated masterpiece has become one of the monuments of the twentieth century and a symbol for all Australia.

The construction of the Opera House seen in 1965 from the base of the monumental staircase.

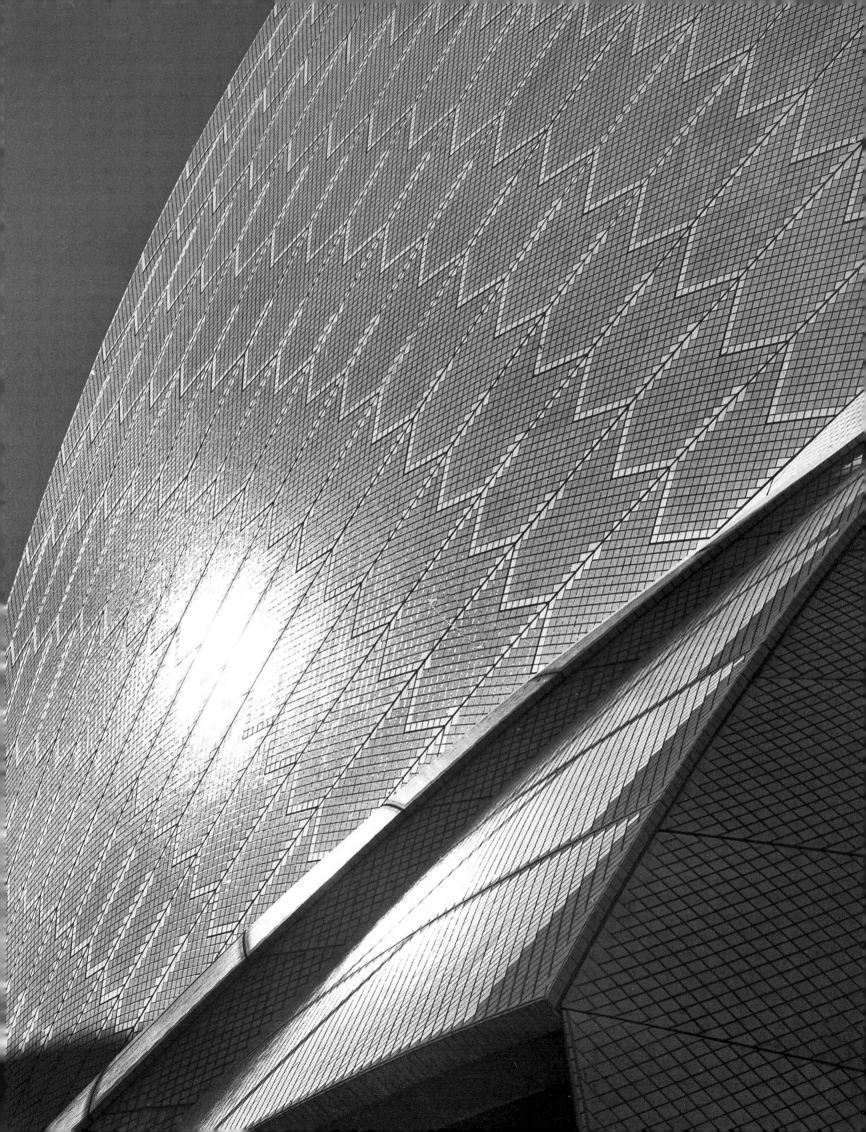

The play of light on the white ceramic tiles, matt and shiny, of the Opera House roof.

Central Sydney photographed by Wolfgang Sievers in 1961.
G. F. Hilly's 1856 Royal Exchange building (left)
was demolished shortly afterward.

From City Centre to Downtown

The decision to build the Opera House on Bennelong Point anticipated the future destiny of the cityscape: by bestowing its prestige onto the city, Utzon's masterpiece catalysed its metamorphosis. In 1957 the state government relaxed regulations limiting the height of buildings to 150 feet (45.7 metres), liberating developers from one of the principal constrictions that had made office blocks less than satisfactory financial investments. The largely nineteenth-century buildings of Circular Quay were torn down and whole city blocks were demolished to be replaced by towers designed in a bland local version of the International Style. There were notable exceptions: Harry Seidler's powerful geometric shafts of concrete alveoli have set a standard of architectural quality that few of his colleagues have achieved. His elegantly cylindrical Australia Square, completed in 1967, and designed in collaboration with the Italian engineer Pier Luigi Nervi, was the first, followed by his MLC Centre in 1978, Grosvenor Tower in 1988 and the Capita Centre in 1990.

Writing in 1963, the architectural historian Morton Herman opined that "the wholesale demolition of the city's Victorian buildings has, and is being, carried out at a pace that can only be described as breathtaking."[84] Little or no protection was offered for nineteenth-century buildings. George McRae's 1893 Queen Victoria Building – now regarded as a jewel in the city's crown – was stigmatised as being "monstrous, antique and an incongruity among the surrounding modern structures ... a glaring example of civic apathy and backwardness."[85] The authorities and organisations responsible for overseeing the preservation of the city's built environment – the minister for planning and the National Trust of Australia (New South Wales)[86] ignored those historic buildings failing to live up to idealised "Georgian colonial" paradigms, particularly if there were favourable financial advantages in the offing. By the end of the 1960s Sydney was well on the way to looking like the American model it had so recently sought to emulate, albeit on a reduced scale and set within a landscape that still, despite all odds, prevailed.

Harbour view from Seidler's office at Milson Point,
designed by the architect in 1971.

Blue's Point Tower, west of the Harbour Bridge, one of Seidler's most
controversial schemes.

The business heart of Sydney changed dramatically during the 1970s.
Seidler's MLC tower is occupying the site of the prestigious Hotel Australia
and the Royal Theatre (1972-78).

This model of a new residential development for McMahon's Point
proposed by Seidler in 1957 was inspired by Walter Gropius planning principles.

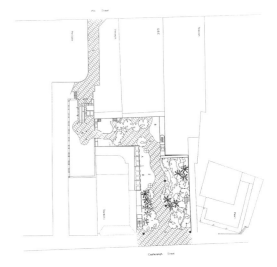

The Capita building, a different type of tower constructed by Seidler during the 1980s, connects two streets by a landscaped walkway traversing a planted atrium.

The architect Hugh Buhrich's house at Castlecrag (1972) is no less than a structural and spatial tour de force perched over one of the coves of Middle Harbour.

Buhrich house: entrance façade, spiral staircase,
dining room, cross section and bathroom
in moulded fibreglass.

The reception spaces at Buhrich house. Highly pronounced over the entrance façade and kitchen, the undulating ceiling gradually levels off towards the other side, opening onto a view of the harbour.

Bondi Beach,
the most celebrated of Sydney's ocean retreats.

The Contemporary City

The appearance of the city today has been determined largely by the Sydney Region Outline Plan 1970-2000, the planning scheme that superceded the 1951 County of Cumberland plan which had regulated the growth of the city up to 1975. By the mid 1960s it had become evident that population projections on which the earlier scheme was based had been far-exceeded. The new masterplan promoted linear growth of the city along a network of transport routes. To free-up the inner city from the pressures of traffic congestion and to allow for the growth of commercial and retail facilities it encouraged the development of motorways, the expansion of suburbs and the formation of a massive conurbation, stretching beyond greater Sydney to absorb the eastern coastal cities of Wollongong to the south and Newcastle to the north. Its underlying aim reflected that of the conservative state government that commissioned it; by expanding into a vast megalopolis Sydney would maintain its position as Australia's pre-eminent capital. Today Sydney is a city of some four million inhabitants, scattered over a surface of 12,500 square kilometres – one of the lowest urban densities in the world.[87] And whereas, until well until the middle of the century, the city's residential population was contained within a grid of nineteenth and early twentieth century Anglophonic suburbs – Paddington, Surry Hills, Glebe, Balmain, Strathfield, Concord and Haberfield – its demographic centre is now to be found in the western suburbs at Lidcombe. And the Central Business District now extends across the harbour into North Sydney and beyond. Limited to the east by the Pacific Ocean the city extends some 100 kilometres westwards, up to the foothills of the Blue Mountains; to the north and south this carpet of suburbs is partially constrained by the two national parks. Less than an hour by road from the city centre these parks are nature preserves on a grand scale, the recreational stamping grounds of a suburban populace seduced by a myth that, as an antidote to the debilitating influences of urban life, it is necessary to immerse oneself in nature periodically.

New Identities

The privileged landscape of the northern beaches of Sydney: Barrenjoey Point separating Pittwater from Palm and Whale Beaches, with Ku-ring-gai National Park in the background.

A popular – if inaccurate – image of Sydney is that of a harbour, fringed by a thin strip of bush, dotted with sandy bays overlooked by the mansions of a few wealthy inhabitants and two iconic structures, the Opera House and the Harbour Bridge. This vision ignores the constant activity taking place, night and day, on the vast, liquid *piazza grande* of the harbour, the disappointing panorama of the inner city – a dense urban blot spiked with an architecture of ubiquitous dullness – as well as the unrelieved tedium of the city's sprawling suburbs, formed by one block of red-tiled houses succeeding another. Likewise, it is only recently that the fiction of the city being populated by the sun-tanned, sturdy and hard-drinking descendants of Anglo-Irish convicts has been dispelled from prevailing perceptions. The end of the Second World War saw an influx of non-British immigrants from Europe; the abandonment of the federal government's white Australia policy in the 1960s saw the arrival of migrants from Turkey and Lebanon, followed in the 1970s and 1980s by refugees from South East Asia and Latin America. The 1990s have seen nearly two fifths of the city's migrants coming from Asian backgrounds. More recently migrants from former Yugoslavia have been added to this cultural melting pot. By 1991 nearly half of Sydney's population comprised of persons from first or second generation non-English speaking backgrounds. And whilst Sydney has always been a city of migrants these postwar influxes have changed the city's ethnic composition beyond recognition. Whole suburbs have at various times been annexed by those speaking a language other than English, living in a manner that has little to do with the traditional suburban culture of white Australia. The official policy of multiculturalism, introduced over the last two decades, has become one of the new values of contemporary Australia. Widely promoted, it not only reflects the growing influence of "political correctness" on public ideology but also helps to ameliorate latent tensions between various communities.

The changes that have been wrought in the way the inner city is perceived – not only by those who view it from outside but also by its inhabitants – date from the early 1970s when, after 23 years of conservative federal government, an Australian Labor Party administration was formed in Canberra. Led by the charismatic Gough Whitlam the new government initiated a short-lived period of cultural release.[88] This renaissance, part of a quest to define national identity and a belated attempt to distance the country from its British colonial origins, prompted a re-evaluation of both the built and natural environments. As Whitlam's minister for the environment observed: "the environment is rather more than just a concern about kangaroos and birds, or tin cans and garbage."[89]

And just as Sydney business began to promote the efficiencies of the International Style in the Central Business District, so the children of the postwar suburbs began to discover the delights of inner city living in a nineteenth-century terrace house, even while these were threatened with the possibility of wholesale demolition. The conservative Liberal-Country Party coalition that had ridden to power in the 1965 state elections was predisposed to the interests of development, to the idea of transforming the city into a modern, dynamic, Americanised, centre of the South Pacific. The terraced inner city suburbs of Paddington and Glebe were threatened by the infiltration of motorways. In 1968 the state government established the Sydney Cove Redevelopment Authority with a remit to demolish what was left of nineteenth-century residential housing in The Rocks and to replace it by terraced office tower blocks. And in 1972 Woolloomooloo was on the cusp of a private redevelopment that "will make a clean sweep of much of the haphazard industrial and residential structures in this magnificently-situated basin … [it] will become, in effect, not only a second front door to Sydney but the port's major ocean passenger terminal."[90] But these dramatic plans had been drawn up without consideration of resident opposition or recognition of the power of certain trade unions.

As early as 1964 a resident action group, the Paddington Society, had been established to prevent the demolition of the suburb. By the 1970s resident action groups were springing up to defend not only houses but also reserves of native bush. In 1971 the Builders' Labourers Federation (BLF), a trade union under the leadership of the dynamic Communist Jack Mundey, instituted an embargo process of environmental activism known as "green bans." Their first ban was imposed on an area of suburban bushland in Hunter's Hill. In a bizarre alliance with the largely middle-class "Battler's for Kelly's Bush" they succeeded in thwarting its subdivision for catalogue housing. The most notable achievements of the green ban movement were the retention of Woolloomooloo and Glebe as working-class housing. In 1974 the federal government purchased the largely run down Glebe Estate from the Church of England and in 1975 acquired large tracts of Woolloomooloo from the, now bankrupt, entrepreneur. The federal government transferred the lands to the New South Wales Housing Commission specifically for low-income housing with a caveat that new building works should be in keeping with the remaining nineteenth century buildings.

Aboriginals in the urban ghetto of Redfern in the early 1980s.

The grid plan of the suburbs constitutes the greater part of Sydney's urban fabric.

Together with a change in attitudes towards the city's architectural heritage, the 1970s heralded a rediscovery of the landscape and its native vegetation and a marked shift in the perception of Aboriginal land rights.[91] The Queensland state government's decision to lease Fraser Island to a sand mining company sparked the beginning of nationwide environmental activism,[92] reflecting a new outlook on the bush that saw it neither as a vast natural resource awaiting exploitation nor as a volatile, malevolent force. In line with this change of attitude, developers began to place a premium on bushland properties. The national parks became magnets for suburban expansion, despite the fact that the houses built on their fringes would be exposed to the fires that devastate the bush during the hot, dry summer months which see the oil-drenched leaves of the eucalyptus trees ignite in seconds.

Living in nature, even to the extent of becoming part of it, is an idea that two of Sydney's best known contemporary architects, Glenn Murcutt and Richard Leplastrier, espouse. They work, almost exclusively, in the field of domestic architecture not only because it suits the small size of their practices but also because the individual scale of this type of work allows them to realise their convictions. As they build houses for selected clients, with whom they share common values and beliefs, their architecture is indissociable from a particular way of life, from a particular approach to the land. Both architects make reference to the painter Lloyd Rees, a teacher and a friend of Leplastrier's. Rees believed that man is shaped by the land, avowing that this could be seen in the symbiotic relationship the Aboriginals have with it. Murcutt and Leplastrier have become the venerated representatives of an architectural "Australianness", a strand of nationalism that Sydney claims to have invented and the existence of which it vehemently defends. Both architects are from the same generation (Murcutt was born in 1936, Leplastrier in 1939) and both began their architectural studies at the time the "Sydney School" became influential

Glenn Murcutt's 1990 Magney house seen against a backdrop of terraced housing in the nineteenth-century suburb of Paddington.

amongst practitioners. Both taught in the Department of Architecture at the University of Sydney during the late 1970s – something they continue to do both in Australia and overseas – influencing through their teaching the work of young architects.

For Murcutt, contemporary Australia is a unique synthesis between a new civilization and an ancient landscape – albeit an inhospitable one – an environment which, for at least 50,000 years, the Aboriginals roamed, investing it with a symbolism of unequalled complexity, before European invasion irretrievably altered the indigenous culture. Murcutt regards the Australian landscape as the common denominator for the country's contemporary multicultural population. His architecture is resolutely contemporary, declaring its man-made character without mimicking natural forms whilst making respect for the environment in which it is built an absolute requirement. Murcutt finds in the landscape of each site the tools for creating the architecture of each building: the path of the sun, the direction of the prevailing winds, its geology and hydrology. The site is revealed through close observation of its condition and by interpretation of clues and details such as the type and distribution of its vegetation and the traces of its groundwater flow. This analysis dictates the positioning of the house, inserted into the landscape in a way that least disturbs it, and determines certain features linked to its climatic efficacy: orientation, the dimension of the awnings, the porosity of the façade and the position of the verandahs.

In the early 1960s Murcutt travelled extensively around the world and he has retained an active memory of the architectures he encountered. Whilst fascinated by traditional Cycladic villages and Cotswold farmhouses his architectural vocabulary was also strongly influenced by European Modernism, notably Mies Van der Rohe's minimalism, particularly as it is expressed in the Farnsworth House (1950), where it confronts the open landscape

Interior view of the Magney house. Walls and openings are organised to conceal other houses, giving a sense of being in nature rather than in a dense residential area.

of North America. His rediscovery of an Australian vernacular heritage – both industrial and agricultural – during the period he was establishing his practice explicitly reoriented his forms toward curved roofs, the use of humble materials, such as timber and corrugated iron, materials favoured in Australian rural buildings during the latter part of the nineteenth century. Drawing on these firmly established principles, Murcutt has designed numerous houses in Sydney and its suburbs which form a constantly evolving variation on a "type" of ideal habitation: long, lightweight pavilions invested with fluid open plans and capped by graceful roofs, all finely attuned to the conditions of climate and locale; houses which, for the first time in the history of Sydney architecture, are influencing those being built in Europe and America. Among the more notable is the house he designed for the painter Syd Ball, located on the edge of the Ku-ring-gai National Park (1983). It is a simple, rectangular pavilion, sheathed in corrugated iron and anchored to the sloping rockface by thin steel pilotis. The main body of the house is connected to the landscape by a delicate wooden lath footbridge and by verandahs giving views over the surrounding

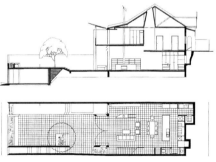

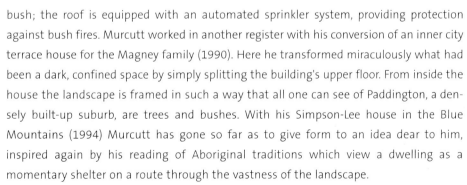

bush; the roof is equipped with an automated sprinkler system, providing protection against bush fires. Murcutt worked in another register with his conversion of an inner city terrace house for the Magney family (1990). Here he transformed miraculously what had been a dark, confined space by simply splitting the building's upper floor. From inside the house the landscape is framed in such a way that all one can see of Paddington, a densely built-up suburb, are trees and bushes. With his Simpson-Lee house in the Blue Mountains (1994) Murcutt has gone so far as to give form to an idea dear to him, inspired again by his reading of Aboriginal traditions which view a dwelling as a momentary shelter on a route through the vastness of the landscape.

During the mid 1960s Leplastrier worked as one of Utzon's assistants; the Danish architect had migrated to Sydney in 1963 to supervise work on the Opera House. Counting on remaining indefinitely, he began work on a house in Bayview, an inlet off Pittwater where Leplastrier then lived and lives now. Like Utzon, he has a passion for sailing and boat building. His discovery of Asian architecture was cemented during a stay in Kyoto in 1963

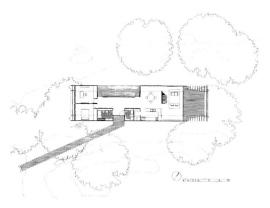

Inhabiting the landscape: the lightweight metallic house designed by Glenn Murcutt in 1983 for the painter Syd Ball at Glenorie, on the boundary of Ku-ring-gai National Park.

House overlooking Pittwater designed by Richard Leplastrier.

where he studied traditional forms of temple construction. These experiences have strongly influenced Leplastrier's architectural universe and explain a number of traits discernible in his work: the inspiration he finds in observing natural phenomena, the talent demonstrated in creating a learned dialogue between building and site and his taste for elevated platforms on which the routines of daily life are transformed into minor rituals. For him the land fashioned by human activity is already architecture, an explicit reference to the Aboriginal way of using the crevices in rocks or branches bent into arched forms and covered with bark to provide shelter which are used then abandoned. Leplastrier is fascinated by the fundamental actions through which humanity has fashioned a place to live in the land and he is one of the few who militantly oppose the – at times, indiscriminate and indifferent – expansion of urban Sydney onto the special geography of this ancient landscape.[93] His own house in Pittwater, designed recently, is accessible only by boat. Its vast communal space, dedicated to family life, is covered with a wide, overhanging roof and illuminated by vast portholes set into the recycled plywood of the lightweight external walls. His houses are crafted objects, superbly realised, often by specialist boatbuilders. Amongst them is the Palm House at Bilgola Beach (1972), an assemblage of precious woods, the mobile elements of which – sliding walls and retractable cloth roof panels – can be opened or closed at will in response to changing climatic conditions to reveal the enclosed garden in which the house is embedded.

109

City Values

In 1976, after eleven years of conservative hegemony, the Australian Labor Party regained power in New South Wales. The new state government had been elected at a time when attitudes to inner city living were changing. The battles for the preservation of suburbs such as Paddington, Woolloomooloo, Glebe and Balmain had sparked new interest in not only preserving the city's nineteenth-century heritage but, increasingly, the middle classes were abandoning the suburbs, opting to live in areas previously avoided as slums. Cognisant of change in both the social geography of the city and public attitudes towards the environment the state government introduced a heritage bill into parliament which provided "a legislative basis for the conservation, enhancement and preservation of the state's environmental heritage ... [which] comprises the buildings, works, relics and places considered to have historic, scientific, cultural and social, archaeological, architectural, natural or aesthetic significance to the State."[94] Fired with enthusiasm the government initiated a programme of conserving and restoring colonial buildings in the administrative precinct of Macquarie Street. It halted the previous administration's grand

A refined use of commonplace materials characterises this 1999 warehouse conversion by the architect Sam Marshall.

plans for interweaving the fabric of the inner city with motorways and began acquiring significant properties and sites with a view to ensuring their continued preservation. The initial enthusiasm of the state government towards heritage matters waned throughout the eighties. It became most obvious in 1983 when the government-controlled State Bank demolished its 1936 headquarters to vocal protest, followed shortly after by the bulldozing through Parliament of an act that exempted the authority it was setting up to control the anticipated bicentennial developments at Darling Harbour from the very

The inserted staircase in Marshall's warehouse conversion is treated both as a window and a piece of sculpture.

In his 1998 Bell house, Sam Marshall creates a symbiosis between living space and the garden.

Berowra Waters, Glenn Murcutt's restaurant on the Hawkesbury River, was converted from an existing teahouse at the end of the 1970s.

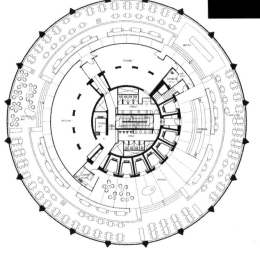

The Summit, a revolving restaurant at the top of Australia Square-one of the first Sydney tower blocks designed by Harry Seidler in 1962- was renovated by Burley Katon Halliday in 1998.

heritage legislation it had so recently introduced and, finally, the near-sale of the First Government House site to developers, the latter action being averted by the discovery of substantial archaeological remains on the site. Meanwhile the building heritage profession became increasingly rigorous in the way it approached the conservation and restoration of buildings and sites. Drawing on a set of principles enunciated in the 1978 ICOMOS Burra Charter, bodies such as the Historic Houses Trust of New South Wales, formed by the state government in the early 1980s, renounced a policy of "restoring" buildings to "ideal" conditions. Emphasis was now placed on restorations based on rigorous physical evidence or, increasingly, on leaving things as they were, merely consolidating whatever existed. Similarly the Historic Houses Trust began to look beyond the old houses of the rich and famous, acquiring former "slum" properties in The Rocks and in 1988 Harry Seidler presented it with the first house he built in Sydney, the Rose Seidler House.

It was against this distinctly urban background that Sydney began to develop a resolutely individualistic culture of pleasure. With its emphasis on comfortable lifestyle the city began during the 1980s to place increasing value on interior architecture and design, on the quality of food, on fashion and the arts. It spawned new shops, boutiques, commercial galleries and restaurants in previously industrial inner city districts. Entire lengths of street underwent transformation. Oxford Street – which runs from Hyde Park near the centre of the city up to the gates of Centennial Park in Paddington – metamorphosed from an endless row of drab, semi-derelict junk shops, butchers and run-down pubs into the lurid "gay mile" (where Sydney's celebrated Gay and Lesbian Mardi Gras – the largest nocturnal outdoor parade in the world – has been held annually since 1978) at the city end and into a assortment of fashionable boutiques, restaurants and antique dealers at the Paddington end. Similar transformations have been wrought throughout other inner city suburbs.

Luigi Rosselli's Mensa restaurant in Paddington
and Synman Justin Bialek's MG Garage in Surry Hills
were both designed in 1998.

The Q bar in Oxford Street. Interior fit out and furniture
by Danny Venlet (1995).

Architecture was recruited to provide a stage for the increasingly sophisticated activities of daily life. Young architects in small practices worked on projects that reflected this hedonistic life, notably on the modification of existing buildings into shops, apartments and bars or on the construction of individual houses, often their own. Whatever the formal obediences of these architects, the greater number of their projects are testimony to a shared belief, that of maintaining in the city a rapport with nature, one that blurs the frontiers between the interior and the exterior, that emphasises the fluidity of generous living spaces which open onto gardens of native and sub-tropical flora, of open balconies and timber-decked terraces. In the hope of obtaining designs that would give their pro-perties fashionable kudos and added financial value, clients allowed their architects considerable freedom and stimulated experimentation. Focus was placed on developing a shared identity of forms, design detail and, not least, the choice of materials and up to the minute furnishings.

Meanwhile restaurants, bars and coffee shops began to acquire new glamour and sophistication. The trend was launched at the end of the 1970s when Tony and Gay Bilson commissioned Glenn Murcutt to convert Berowra Waters Inn, a former tearoom on the Hawkesbury River, into a restaurant. One hour north of the city by road and considerably less by private flying boat the restaurant rapidly acquired renown throughout the world not only for the quality of its food and the beauty of its surrounding landscape but also for the originality of the architecture.[95] Tony Bilson transferred the concept into the inner city in the early 1980s when he commissioned Murcutt and the design firm Marsh Freedman to transform the Bruce Dellit designed Charles Kinsela Funeral Parlour (1933) into a

Running from the city to Centennial Park, Oxford Street is today one of the city's more lively environs.

brasserie restaurant. Dellit's dramatic chapel was given a wash of bright colours and a former coffin storage room was converted into a canary yellow bar. The restaurant's success prompted a rash of imitations throughout the city, many designed by former employees of Marsh Freedman. Celebrity chefs and restaurateurs have recruited designers to create spectacular visual and spatial experiences to complement the pleasures of their tables, as new Australian cuisine makes reference to Asia not only in terms of taste but also in focusing on the arts of presentation. In the incestuous world of interior architecture the firm Burley Katon Halliday, one of the veterans of renovation chic, is distinguished by its – sometimes flashy – opulent minimalism. Its work includes a number of restaurants. For the Darley Street Thai (1993), they have married an exotic fusion of sophisticated colour with lacquered and gilded surfaces. And for the noodle bar at Sailor's Thai (1995), a former soup kitchen in The Rocks – now renovated into Sydney's tourist ghetto – they have created a space that wraps "un-heritage" bronze-coloured ceilings and walls around a vast stainless steel bench matched with Thonet chairs. Most recently the firm has rendered The Summit, a revolving restaurant at the top of Seidler's 1968 Australia Square, with a brightly coloured 1960s aesthetic.

Over a twenty-year period the collaboration between restaurateurs and designers has given birth to numerous well-known venues: Anders Ousback's Wharf restaurant at Walsh Bay, designed in 1986 by Vivian Fraser, the Burdekin public bar for Nigel Hannigan and Bart Gitmans, designed in 1989 by Daffodil (Danny Venlet, Marc Newson and Tina Engelen) and Leigh Prentice's 1994 renovation of the Bennelong restaurant at the Opera House for Gay Bilson. The laid-back lifestyle of Sydney, along with the seemingly endless opportunities of working in the field of design, has attracted a number of young architects from outside the city. Amongst them the Italian Luigi Rosselli – a former assistant of Mario Botta who arrived in Sydney in 1985 – has since designed numerous bars and restaurants throughout the city, particularly for the Italian community. The urge to experiment has resulted in original places created by the hybridisation of conventionally distinct functions; one of the more recent examples being Fuel, a combination of a food store, restaurant and bar with a showroom for classic cars, installed like sculptures between the tables of the restaurant, designed by the Melbourne-based firm Justin Bialek Synman in 1998.

If the Sydney-based interior architecture and design phenomenon had provided hot copy for international design magazines[96] and had been used to promote the idea of a creative Australia by federal authorities then the same could not be said for much of the architecture forming the city's contemporary urban landscape. The brutality and sheer banality of much of the Central Business District results, in part, from the fragmentation of planning controls and a failure by the city's numerous authorities to develop a cohesive urban vision, a situation hardly unique to Sydney. Planning in Sydney is controlled at local level by various municipalities who work within limited legislative parameters. Local municipalities remain the "consent" authorities although they are subject to ministerial intervention. At a regional level authority is held by the state government who exercises its considerable powers through, notably, the Department of Public Works and Services – with its army of architectural civil servants – along with the Department of Urban Affairs and Planning and numerous other authorities and advisory bodies, often with overlapping powers.[97] At a national level the federal government – based in Canberra – is implicated in a number of decisions concerning the city's infrastructure, and in respect of current debates – through its ownership of a number of redundant military sites around Port Jackson – it is playing an increasingly important role. The rivalries between the various layers of government and the incoherence engendered by this antagonism is being exploited by an all-powerful private sector seemingly setting the agenda for the city's development.

The Wharf restaurant in one of the Walsh Bay finger wharves was converted by Vivian Frazer (1986).

The Bel Mondo restaurant by Luigi Rosselli.

Bicentennial Festivities

The numerous schemes planned for the bicentennial established an urban policy that mixed massive incursions into the city's redundant industrial infrastructure with a programme of selective improvement in the public domain, implemented through superficial interventions pointedly aimed at the tourist and leisure industry. The architecture of the bicentennial, dominated as it was by the government architect's office and the larger Sydney firms gives a, perhaps too, revealing picture of what architecture in Sydney was about in the 1980s. The Australian Bicentennial was as much about Sydney as it was about European settlement of the continent. Smaller beanfeasts had been held in 1888 (the centenary of European settlement), in 1901 (federation of the states) and most recently in 1970 to commemorate the bicentenary of Cook's exploration of the eastern coast of Australia.[98] By contrast 1988 was to be the mother of all celebrations, an antipodean echo of the 1976 Bicentenary of the American Revolution with the added extras of visits by British royalty, a major cricket series and a tall ships regatta in Sydney Harbour. Responding to a growing sense of cultural hubris, it was intended as a jubilatory glance at two hundred years of achievement: in the words of the inevitable jingle a "celebration of a nation" – cynics dubbed it the "masturbation of a nation."

In Sydney, the bicentennial programme, largely directed by the state government, was planned around a number of *grands projets*, enduring monuments that would not only

The industrial wasteland of Darling Harbour-the cradle of Australian industry-as it appeared following the clearance of the rail and port facilities in 1984.

Darling Harbour was transformed into a commercial theme park masquerading as public space. In the foreground, from left to right: the Australian National Maritime Museum, the market building, the Convention Centre, the western distributor and the Sydney Exhibition Centre. Photographed in 1995.

provide tangible evidence of the event but which would also relieve unemployment. These included the rehabilitation of existing cultural institutions, the creation of new sports facilities, the development of tourist amenities and the recuperation of Darling Harbour, Sydney's main working point until 1971 when it was moved to Botany Bay. In 1984 it was announced that Darling Harbour would be redeveloped as the state's major contribution to the bicentennial festivities. It would encompass an exhibition building, a convention centre, a park, a foreshore promenade, a Chinese garden, a new National Maritime Museum, a "people mover" system and commercial developments such as hotels and, controversially, a casino. In order to achieve this within the restricted time available Darling Harbour was to be controlled by a statutory authority, the Darling Harbour Authority, and exempted from state and municipal planning legislation and regulation.[99] The government stipulated that the design and development arms of the authority be private firms and that a significant *tranche* of capital for the project be provided by private enterprise. The 64-hectare site was partially built on reclaimed land, it was prone to flooding, littered with heritage items of varying significance including the disconnected Pyrmont Bridge and, over-shadowed by the partly-built flyover, the western distributor. Pedestrian access was difficult and there were no existing transport connections. A strategy for design and construction was developed by the Authority, initially in collaboration with the Department of Public Works. Significantly, a decision was taken to give

The Overseas ol on the western flank of Circular Quay
was renovated by Lawrence Nield & Partners for the Bicentenary.

Bisecting façades and obscuring vistas,
the Monorail crosses George Street, 1988.

Bicentennial illuminations in Macquarie Street
designed by the Department of Public Works.

The "roller coaster", the Sydney Football Stadium
in Moore Park designed by Philip Cox Richardson
& Taylor in 1985.

priority to construction deadlines over design considerations. The template adopted for the planning aped similar waterfront developments in the United States, in particular that of the Baltimore Inner Harbor Redevelopment.

The market building, a privately funded scheme, was based on similar structures developed in America by the Rouse Corporation; its design reflected its content: fast food restaurants and souvenir shops. The convention centre was designed by John Andrews International, a firm founded by the Canadian-based Australian architect John Andrews. Formed around a semi-circular auditorium it is ringed by a series of eight *in situ* cast concrete circular stairwells. It is an awkward lump of a building, wedged between the pylons of an expressway, framed against a multi-storey parking lot and abutting the ephemeral barrel vaulting of the market building. The casino-hotel project failed to proceed in time for the Bicentennial due to the "discovery" that one of the operators proposed for the complex had been involved in legally questionable activities. It was just one of the many controversies surrounding the redevelopment. The exhibition building, the maritime museum and, eventually, the aquarium were all designed by Philip Cox Richardson Taylor & Partners, a large Sydney firm responsible for the design of the nearby University of Technology's Market campus. All three buildings feature tubular steel structures, a rapid build technology that, with the exception of the concrete Convention Centre, is ubiquitous to the buildings erected in Darling Harbour.

The monorail was the most intrusive manifestation of the Darling Harbour redevelopment and, undoubtedly the most controversial. Perched on a high steel rail running through the streets of the southern central business district it was intended to overcome the isolation of the site and connect it into existing public transport facilities. Its appearance in the streets of Sydney provoked outraged demonstrations by a significant minority of the citizenry of Sydney, not to mention the Council of the City of Sydney – the council's protestations may well have contributed to its sacking by the state government in 1987. Running at awning height, the monorail bisects façades and terminates street vistas. Extraordinarily too, the location of the stations fails to coincide with those of the State Rail Authority and a number of them were located on vacant building sites. The much-vaunted "people mover" has become a loss-making toy for tourists whilst an integrated light rail system, similar to that proposed by opponents of the monorail, is being quietly developed to serve not only Darling Harbour but also the inner western suburbs.

In a landscaped park with ready access to the foreshore, Darling Harbour was an immediate popular success although the market place proved initially to be a commercial failure. As politicians have long since recognised, the citizens of Sydney both use and appreciate public parks. Earlier celebrations had resulted in Centennial Park, a haven of open green expanse. By contrast Darling Harbour is a contrived commercial facility masquerading as public space, ringed by towering hotels, overshadowed by unsightly flyovers and, ultimately, a denial of its harbourside location.

Amongst its other projects the government embarked on a programme of installing commemorative monuments in strategic places throughout the city. One such example is the Federation Pavilion in Centennial Park (1984), designed by Alexander Tzannes with murals on the interior of its cupola by the neo-expressionist painter Imants Tiller. The only major bicentennial scheme in Sydney to result from a competition, it is an exercise in patchily understood historicism, a squashed-up bandstand of a building, a form reflecting all too appropriately the brazenly nationalistic tone of the celebrations. The development of sporting facilities and the renovation of cultural institutions was another facet of this programme of *grands projets*. In the early 1970s rumours abounded in Sydney that it would be the favoured site for the 1988 Olympic Games. An Olympic Stadium, along with

The 1988 redevelopment of the approaches to the Sydney Opera House by the Deaprtment of Public Works compromised Utzon's vision for east Circular Quay.

ancillary facilities, was proposed for Moore Park. As it happened the games went to Seoul and only the Sydney Football Stadium (1985) designed by Philip Cox, Richardson & Taylor survived a plethora of protest and the failure of the city to satisfactorily influence the Olympic Committee in its favour. It accommodates almost 40,000 spectators; its curved roof, engineered by Ove Arup & Partners, is supported on a series of tubular steel trusses which carry the weight of the roof down concrete-encased stanchions. Described locally as the Sydney "roller coaster" it is Cox's most visually arresting structure. Responsibility for the design of the extensions to the Art Gallery of New South Wales and the State Library of New South Wales was placed in the hands of the assistant government architect, Andrew Andersons.

Another missed opportunity to give the city a contemporary museum worthy of the name – in spite of the government's stated ambitions – was demonstrated with the redevelopment of the Museum of Applied Arts and Sciences as the Powerhouse Museum. In 1979, it was decided to house the museum in a new venue, the redundant Ultimo Power House and Lionel Glendenning of the government architect's office was appointed principal architect. His solution was to attach a tubular steel-framed demi-barrel vaulted structure to the existing immense double pile brick power house and to clad it with corrugated roofing painted in modish post-modern colours. A modest entrance opens onto a paved *piazza* on the busy Harris Street side of the complex. The design was an attempt at bravura performance, possibly; a misreading of the site and an incomprehension of the museum's function, probably. The building was awarded the Royal Australian Institute of Architects Sulman Prize for 1988.

Much of the bicentennial infrastructure was developed with an eye to the burgeoning tourist market, particularly that drawn from the Asia-Pacific region. During the 1980s a number of large international hotels were erected in the area around Circular Quay which, combined with the reinvention of The Rocks as a tourist precinct, made the rundown condition of the harbour foreshore increasingly apparent. In 1983 the state government directed Andrew Andersons to act as as urban design consultant with a brief to improve the civic design quality of the precinct. On Circular Quay East, ignoring Utzon's 1961 project,[100] he erected a new seawall along Sydney Cove, forming a partly-submerged commercial promenade, connected back to the centre by a glazed tubular steel walkway painted a shade of "degraded red", a colour chosen to echo the – non-Utzonian – Opera House mullions. At central Circular Quay the architects Allan Jack + Cottier stripped out

the ground level installations of the shabby Circular Quay railway station, part of the looming Cahill Expressway (1956), replacing them with restaurants and cafés which opened onto the harbourside promenade. The ferry wharves were re-clad and the pavement was re-laid. It was a simple but effective programme of works. The opening up of the station allowed views onto the harbour while still retaining a maritime atmosphere, and the introduction of restaurants and bars gave life to a part of the city formerly deserted after business hours. At Circular Quay West the promenade fronting the Maritime Services Board building (1940-52) – then being converted into the Museum of Contemporary Art – was extended and the Overseas Passenger Terminal (1961) was redesigned by Lawrence Nield & Partners who partially demolished and re-clad the structure. It is one of the successes in the redefinition of the quay. Finally Macquarie Street, one of the few streets in Sydney graced with impressive vistas and a cohesive group of historic buildings had, by the 1980s, become in the words of one Department of Public Works report "less memorable than would be expected."[101] To complement the refurbishment of these heritage buildings a scheme to beautify the street, under the supervision of the government architect's office, saw the footpath widened and paved with manganese red bricks, trees planted and new street furniture installed – designed by Conybeare Morrison & Partners – complete with lollipop street lights and bus shelters evoking nineteenth-century trams. Concurrent with this much-publicised work the government quietly leased Mortimer Lewis's 1849 Treasury Building to the Intercontinental Hotel chain who adapted it for hotel purposes and erected a twenty-eight-storey tower in the process.[102] The street was a backdrop for a series of spectacular decorative arches, devised by the Department of Public Works, and erected for the duration of the celebrations.

The bicentennial was intended as an act of celebration, a commemoration of Sydney's two hundred years of white history, as an indicator of Australia's new found sense of national identity and creativity. It was also a calculated political move designed to create a "feel good factor" amongst a populace struggling with a precarious local economy. Summing it up, the novelist Patrick White bemoaned: "Circuses don't solve serious problems. When the tents are taken down, we'll be left with the dark, the emptiness – and probably a two-dollar loaf."[103]

129

Railway Square

Trains
Shops
TAFE
Subway to
George and Lee Streets

The redevelopment of Railway Square as a rail-bus interchange by the Department of Public Works and Services and the City of Sydney (City Projects).

The underground connection between Central Railway Station and the new rail bus interchange.

Urban Affairs

Newspaper kiosk, Martin Place, one of the elements of the new street furniture designed by the Cox Group for J. C. Decaux International.

The bicentennial had prompted the authorities into a frenzy of refurbishment and redecoration of the city. The designation of Sydney as the venue for the 27th Olympiad in 1993 resulted in a similar frenzy. In 1997, in anticipation both of the third millennium and the forthcoming games, the City of Sydney launched an unprecedented capital works programme aimed at improving its urban spaces and creating a range of cultural and sporting facilities. In conjunction with the Department of Public Works and Services it has reconstructed the bus/rail interchange at Railway Square, adjacent to the Central Railway Station and, in an attempt to homogenise the appearance of the cityscape, is refurbishing parks, repaving footpaths and malls and has let contracts for a new range of street furniture designed by the architects Cox Richardson for Jean-Claude Decaux International. The former Customs House on Circular Quay has been transformed into a cultural information centre and its surroundings have been completely redesigned. Other schemes include two sport and recreation centres and a reconstructed harbourside pool.

It is perhaps surprising, given its all-embracing powers, how very few buildings of quality have resulted from the state government's architectural policies, even when implemented through the city's leading architectural practices. Recent schemes undertaken by the Department of Public Works and Services include a major refurbishment of the New South Wales Conservatorium of Music — built around the remnants of Greenway's 1817 Gothic Government House stables — in the Botanic Gardens. The government's redevelopment of the site has been criticised by the National Trust for "swamping the original building and endangering an early roadway and drainage channels."[104] The government architect's

The atrium inserted behind the façade of the former Sydney Customs House was transformed into a cultural information centre by the architects Tonkin Zulaikha in collaboration with Jackson Teece Chesterman & Willis and City Projects.

design strips the Greenway building of recent accretions, transferring their accommodation into buildings partially entombed into the surrounding terrain which, at the Macquarie Street end of the site, rise up to form an high terracotta block. The furore over the future of the site seems to have resulted not only from the clumsiness of the design and a gung-ho attitude to heritage issues but also from the government's attempts to conceal the scale of structures being added from premature public scrutiny.[105]

Despite the avowed intention of the government architect to promote a practice "that is part of the universal thrust of architecture in cities, but with a local characteristic and local flavour"[106] a number of few schemes aimed at boosting the international image of Sydney as a centre for contemporary architecture have been held. In 1997 an invited competition for the second stage of the Museum of Contemporary Art at Circular Quay selected Kazuyo Sejima, one of the rising stars of the Japanese scene, to undertake the design of its Cinematheque. For the first time since Utzon a foreign architect of renown has been retained to create a major public building in the city. And in 1996, taking advantage of the growing sale of public assets by the state government, a consortium of developers Lend Lease, Mirvac and the East Asia Property Group acquired the redundant State Office Block (1967),[107] demolished it and commissioned Renzo Piano to design a double tower of deluxe apartments and offices, "Aurora Place". Indubitably, the glassy, flower-like forms with

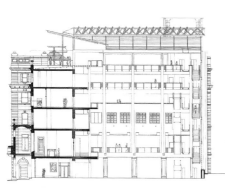

The renovated façade of James Barnet's 1887
Customs House and a cross section of the new atrium.

The IBM tower (Stephenson & Turner, 1964)
before and after its conversion into luxury
apartments by Crone & Associates.

which the Genoese architect has wrapped the building will become one of the landmarks of the city, all the more so since these new towers with their louvred façades and terracotta cladding are being presented as a model of ecologically sustainable architecture. Other sales of public assets have resulted in less notable results. Countless public buildings and sites have been sold off to private investors by state and federal governments alike and redeveloped in order to satisfy the requirements of business and tourism. The reckless demolitions of the 1960s and early 1970s have been succeeded by a new phase of mass readaptation of noteworthy buildings, of entire blocks, often situated in the most sensitive parts of the city. Other private companies have not been slow to seize on the advantages to be gained from recruiting prestigious signatures: the British telecommunications company BT plc has signed up the London-based architects Foster and Partners (along with the local firm Hassell Architects) for a new tower block on Phillip Street. Warnings from heritage bodies are more often than not dismissed as governments, both conservative and labor, both federal and state, rewrite or bypass heritage laws to ensure the sale of the city's public patrimony. James Barnet's monumental General Post Office in the symbolic heart of the city, Martin Place, has been decked out with an incongruous high-rise block during its transformation into a hotel and offices. And, after being repeatedly threatened with demolition, the Woolloomooloo finger wharf – the longest timber construction in the southern hemisphere – has been partially demolished and divided into luxury apartments and an hotel by the developers Multiplex/Walker; the redevelopment has been accompanied by the construction of a marina/apartment complex inserted into the ridge that forms the eastern boundary of the Botanic Gardens. The finger wharves at Walsh Bay along with their associated port buildings, are now being subjected to redevelopment under the guise of "adaptive re-use" by developers in a deal brokered by the Department of Public Works and Services. Once considered significant enough to be proposed for World Heritage listing, this unique harbourside complex is being selectively demolished and the spoils allocated between cultural and commercial interests; the creation of deluxe apartments professedly funding the so-called "public" facilities.

The cosmetic changes wrought by updating the appearance of buildings under the pretext of change of use concern public as well as private, significant nineteenth-century as well as quite ordinary twentieth-century buildings. The powerful neo-classical massing of the Customs House has been capped with a new glass roof whilst its interior has been hollowed out to form a central atrium during its transformation into a cultural information centre complete with an Aboriginal art gallery and a "modern restaurant capturing sweeping views of Sydney Harbour."[108] On Kent Street the former IBM building, designed in 1964 by Stephenson & Turner and formerly highly regarded[109] has been rendered totally unrecognisable by its transformation into two hundred luxury apartments. Ten storeys and heavy pastiche Modernist balconies have been grafted onto its core and the whole coated with a sombre green and black colour scheme, giving rise to it being dubbed "the stealth bomber."

Even the Opera House has been swept into this frenzy of renovation. In 1998 the Opera House Trust advertised for expressions of interest from experienced project managers and architects in developing a masterplan that would "address practical limitations affecting the function of the building as a performing arts centre. These issues include acoustics in the performing spaces, lighting, visitor amenities and the need to improve access to the building for all visitors, in particular those who are disabled."[110] In plain language the plan was "all about accessibility – oh, and turning a quid."[111] Meanwhile the approach to the building from Circular Quay had been sold to developers as part of a

Contextual model and elevation of Renzo Piano's Aurora Place twin towers on Macquarie Street (1996-2000).

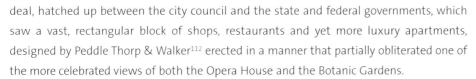

deal, hatched up between the city council and the state and federal governments, which saw a vast, rectangular block of shops, restaurants and yet more luxury apartments, designed by Peddle Thorp & Walker[112] erected in a manner that partially obliterated one of the more celebrated views of both the Opera House and the Botanic Gardens.

Luxury apartment buildings are being constructed at a phenomenal rate throughout the inner city, a growth partly attributable to the interest of Asian investors in the Sydney property market. Seidler, faithful to his belief in the rightness of high-rise construction, has designed a 43-storey apartment building – "Horizon" – in the heart of inner city Darlinghurst. Completed in 1998 the building has aroused controversy, being praised for its response to the problems of urban density but criticised for being out of scale with the neighbourhood and isolated from the street.[113]

At infrastructure level considerable capital investment is being made by the state government, determining the directions of any future growth and development of the city. The construction of a joint rail and tollway link from the city to its principal airport at Mascot on Botany Bay – which includes a massive tunnelling programme under the inner eastern suburbs – has dashed the hopes of those seeking to reduce the number of vehicles in the inner city, as well as thwarting the aspirations of those working to remove the international terminal to the outlying suburbs at Badgery's Creek. This move was violently opposed by pressure groups linked to the tourist industry. Furthermore, in anticipation of

Harry Seidler's Horizon apartment tower, seen from Woolloomooloo.
The curved balconies have glazed guard rails allowing them the benefit of spectacular views over the harbour.

the Olympic Games, the national and international terminals at Mascot have been significantly expanded. The areas serviced by these airport links have become centres for renewed expansion, and the South Sydney Development Corporation – an arm of the Department of Urban Affairs and Planning – is overseeing massive redevelopments around Moore Park. These include a cinematic theme park adjacent to the Fox film studios recently opened on the former Sydney Showgrounds by Rupert Murdoch's News Corporation – an increasingly prominent player in Sydney's burgeoning development industry –[114] and a massive housing redevelopment of the former AGM factory to designs by Denton Corker Marshall, the Melbourne-based firm now with a high commercial profile in Sydney. In a linked development a tunnel is being built under Hyde Park, extending the western distributor through the city and connecting it to the eastern suburbs and the airport. New rail links have been proposed: one connecting Parramatta in the west to Chatswood in the north through the campus of the rapidly expanding Macquarie University, and another extending the Eastern Suburbs railway through to Bondi Beach, a public-private partnership that is arousing a level of local protest reminiscent of earlier community actions.

Internal and external views of the Cook and Phillip Park aquatic centre designed by the architects Bligh Voller Nield.
Note the spires in the background (designed by the same firm) being added to the towers of Wardell's St. Mary's Cathedral.

The Olympics and After

Sydney has been hankering for Olympic Games of its own since the early 1950s when Melbourne was selected as the site for the 1956 event. In the late 1970s the city proffered a bid for the 1988 games – to coincide with the Bicentennial – which they proposed holding at Moore Park in the inner city; it was held in Seoul. In the mid 1980s a preliminary bid was submitted to the Australian Olympic Committee seeking their support to hold the 1996 games at Homebush Bay; they chose to back a failed bid by Melbourne. Finally in 1993 Sydney succeeded in persuading the International Olympic Committee that it had all the infrastructure, all the funding and all the support necessary to host the 27th Olympiad. The reaction was unprecedented, crowds thronged the streets in the early hours of the morning when the news was announced. If the citizens of Sydney had shown a penchant for mass celebration during the Bicentennial, then the Olympics would be the mother of all festivities in a city obsessed by the cult of the body.

The Olympic site under construction. The city centre rises in the distance to the east.

The main setting for these games was again Homebush Bay, twelve kilometres west of the Central Business District in the demographic centre of the Sydney region.[115] This 760-hectare site of partially reclaimed salt marsh and mud flat lies in the upper reaches of the harbour as it enters the Parramatta River. It has been used for a number of industrial purposes including a waste dump (the levels of soil and water pollution were abnormally high), the main city abattoir (described in 1923 as the "worlds largest single killing unit")[116] and the state brickworks all of which closed in 1988. In the mid-1980s the state government began redeveloping part of the former abattoir holding yards as the State Sports Centre intending to convert the remainder into parkland and showgrounds along with retail, commercial and residential facilities. During the same period a new freeway linking Sydney to Parramatta was opened, running adjacent to the site. In 1988 an 100 hectare recreational facility, Bicentennial Park, was opened. Following defeat of the Australian Labor Party state government soon after, a masterplan for the full site was developed – in 1990 – which proposed three staged redevelopment options. One would have flooded the brickpits forming two lakes "suitable for a variety of water-based activities. Another advocated dredging the mouth of Haslam's Creek and flooding only one brickpit. The third possibility envisaged extensive foreshore development while retaining larger stretches of mangrove wetlands, an option declared to be the most environmentally sound proposal.[117] Ultimately though, environmental issues played a relatively small part in these proposals; the overweening aim was to attract private finance to ensure that the Olympic bid had a chance of success.

In 1992 a competition was held for the Olympic Village – part of the move to construct the bid – which attracted 103 entries. The competition brief required the development of affordable medium-density housing with consideration being given for adequate car-parking spaces, social understanding, energy efficiency and care for the built and natural heritage.[118] It aimed at developing a new urban model for Sydney in an attempt to address the increasingly problematic issue of urban sprawl. No single proposal emerged as a winner, and the jury awarded prizes to a short list of seven teams who undertook to find a single solution to the issue – one of the winners was endorsed by Greenpeace.

View looking west. In the foreground is the Silverwater industrial zone abutting
Newington with the Olympic Village to the right, Haslam Creek and the Olympic stadia.

It was becoming increasingly evident that environmental issues would be critical in attracting a favourable decision from the International Olympic Committee. This led to a drastic re-think of the masterplan for site. Sydney's final bid laid stress on the idea that the games would be environmentally sustainable "citing five areas of concern: global warming, ozone depletion,[119] biodiversity, pollution and resource depletion." The environmental sustainability of the bid relied heavily on the green credentials of the Olympic Village proposals. The government declared that: "Homebush Bay is the largest amalgamated site in the centre of the largest city in Australia. It will be the Olympic City in October 2000, and following the Games; a city for 2001: a genuine urban centre for the twenty-first century."[120] The rhetoric was of little account, finally, and the Olympic Village site was sold to developers[121] for "commercial reasons." The weaknesses of the masterplan became increasingly evident as it became obvious that for all its grand intentions Homebush Bay would become just another public-private development, rather like Darling Harbour a decade earlier; developer lead, with cost being the critical factor.

In an attempt to defuse potential criticism the government's Property Services Group extended invitations to a handful of international "big name" architects – Jean Nouvel, Edith Girard, Rem Koolhaas and Renzo Piano (the latter two refused) – along with a selection of local "experts" seeking their participation in a widely-publicised $500,00 Urban Design Studio workshop. Issues concerning the design of the main sports arenas and halls were excluded as were existing facilities.[122] The external massing, siting and urban language of the stadium, the Velodrome, Tennis Centre and Coliseum (now named the Sydney SuperDome)[123] could be addressed. The participants in the workshop were required to address the programmes and the possible ways of linking the different zones in such a way as to transform this collection of sporting facilities into "a genuine urban centre". The results of this brainstorming exercise have never been made public, but it is evident that a number of the ideas put forward have found some resonance in subsequent schemes.

Shortly after the workshop, the Liberal-National Party State government – the promoters of this strategy – were defeated in an election. The Homebush Bay Corporation was then abolished and replaced by the Olympic Co-ordination Authority. A new masterplan was promulgated: it proposed "a core of dense development and a network of roads and other infrastructure ... organised around existing buildings, and took the remnant vegetation and roadways of the grid of abattoir paddocks as an ordering device."[124] In doing so it split the site into three components: the 250-hectare Olympic City, including the Royal Agricultural Society showgrounds that were in the process of being moved from Moore Park; the Olympic Village which would be advanced as a model for future suburban subdivision within the greater Sydney region; and Millennium Park – an extension of Bicentennial Park – which would see the mangrove wetlands retained substantially and the site systematically detoxified. The major stadia would complement the existing sporting facilities and would be constructed by developers using a design and build process of procurement, a form of development that "enables the Olympic authorities and thus the New South Wales government to no longer be the client, to shed responsibility – financial, design and otherwise – 'to shift any risk-taking away from themselves.'"[125] The state government through the Olympic Coordination Authority would be responsible for the infrastructure (the roads, amenities buildings, signage), the detoxification and development of the park and, through the State Rail Authority, the rail link servicing the Olympic City connecting it into the city's rail network.

To co-ordinate the various elements of the design, both existing and proposed, the government brought in the American landscape architects, Hargreaves Associates, this notwithstanding the New South Wales government architect's earlier edict that "foreign architects were a no-no for the Olympic development."[126] Hargreaves attempted to break down the virtual fences surrounding each of the schemes by establishing a two-kilometre long and 170-metre wide boulevard, one ostensibly recalling that at Teotihuacan in Mexico.[127] The boulevard and its associated 9.1-hectare piazza are intended to "unify the site and give it a sense of special scale",[128] cater for crowds and address the larger stadia. The boulevard has been planted with native fig trees along with exotic jacaranda and Manchurian pear trees "chosen for their spectacular spring-time blossoms and cultural importance to Sydney"[129] whilst the plaza has 30-metre-high solar-powered lighting towers. Other features dotting the site include fountains, public art and an entrance "arch", designed by the American James Carpenter, formed of two 30-metre-high masts where "wafting light will be reflected in clouds of mist ... which is all about connecting with nature, the environment and the broad landscape of the site."[130]

The Olympic Park railway station, a long, open-ended, bivalve-shaped building, designed by Hassell Architects, is the principal public access route to the venue. Capable of dealing with around 40,000 persons per hour, its design is intended as a lure to seduce the Sydney public away from the car as its predominant mode of transportation (notwithstanding the provision of a $63 million car park adjacent to the central piazza). Other public transport facilities have been developed, including a new ferry wharf, designed by Alexander Tzannes & Associates, on the Parramatta River, some 3.5 kilometres from the site that will be restricted to VIPs for the duration of the Olympics. A much-vaunted aspect of the design process has been the commissioning of fashionable young architectural practices to design some of the smaller schemes. Indubitably it was a bid to avoid the criticisms that had been levelled at the state's Bicentennial schemes, as big projects dominated by big firms and the New South Wales government architect's office had failed to reflect the range and experimental nature of the local scene. This initiative has produced interesting results, notably the Durbach Block Murcutt Amenities building and the Archery Park designed by Stutchbury & Pape. Yet architects such as Harry Seidler who have put Sydney on the architectural world map, or those who have developed those very aspects of Sydney architecture "lightweight, open-ended design", flaunted in the games propaganda – Glenn Murcutt, Richard Leplastrier and Wendy Lewin – are nowhere represented.

Environmental issues have been a positive driving force behind not only the Olympic developments but also other state government infrastructure projects, spin-offs of the Olympic scheme. Environmental issues have been dealt with coherently and properly: the site has been decontaminated, a process involving the consolidation and capping of waste and the "greening-up" of the site leading to the eventual rehabilitation wetlands environment. An ambitious water reclamation scheme for the buildings and the site as a whole. An energy conservation plan, aiming at reducing the use of energy derived from non-renewable sources has been a determinant in the building programme as has an effective waste reduction strategy. Indeed a recent report by Greenpeace gave the Olympic programme, as a whole, a B-minus rating, whilst noting "a real commitment to environmental guidelines."[131] In part this environmental stance can be perceived quite properly as a marketing tool, an eagerness to give the Sydney games the uniquely identifiable tag of the "green games." But it also forms part of a nationalist agenda, one that locates environment as the determinant influence on the architecture of place. Both the New South Wales government architect and the Royal Australian Institute of Architects have chosen to stress the "Australianness" of the environmental architecture they have promoted."[132]

But the real failure of the Olympic programme lies in its inability to address adequately issues such as quality of design, accessibility, "long-term legacy use" and the problems of an ever expanding suburbia. The Olympic Village should have been a prototype for

145

Aerial and ground views of the new Homebush Bay ferry terminus
on the Parramatta River, designed by Alexander Tzannes, 1998.

The Sydney Showgrounds main arena was designed by the Cox Group.

Opposite page, top:

Stadium Australia designed by the Anglo-Australian firm Bligh Lobb Sports is adjacent
to the Olympic Boulevard (Hargreaves Associates) with its giant solar-powered lighting pylons (Tonkin Zulaikha).

The Archery Centre (Stutchbury & Pape).

Fig Grove and its fountains (Hargreaves Associates) and, in the background, the SuperDome (Cox Richardson with

SECTION D-D

future projects in greater Sydney, yet it is located two kilometres away from the nearest rail link and early efforts to develop it as medium density housing have been discarded in favour of a financially-viable, typically-suburban, commercial housing scheme. The future of the stadia is determined by their commercial viability. As with the bicentennial that preceded it, the New South Wales government's policy toward the games was predicated on an assumption that facilities suitable for a commercial festival can be mistaken for a visionary urban project. On both occasions an event – by definition ephemeral – has been hitched to the future of the whole city. Sydney has every reason to mistrust future pre-texts for those endlessly arising celebrations, the next being in 2001 when the city will be invited to celebrate the centenary of federation, the birth of the Australian nation.

Sydney is a city that, despite its attractions, has yet to invent the urban form that its extraordinary landscape deserves. As the century ends, the observations made by the architect W. Hardy Wilson in the late 1920s – just as the landmarks of Modernism were being raised in Europe – still seem, with notable exceptions, apposite: "The beauty of Sydney does not lie in its buildings. Outside the city, with a multitude of little blue bays, lay the harbour, which was a beautiful spot, and the people had done little to improve it. Where streets were made or buildings erected round the waterside, they were poor things in relation to their surroundings. But wherever parks or gardens were made a feeling for beauty was planted ... Perhaps in another century or two Sydney may become a finished city, filled with splendid buildings ... a new world."[133]

The Olympic Park Railway Station (Hassell Architects).

The amenities building for the Olympic site was designed
by Durbach Block in association with Nick Murcutt.

Following pages:

Sydney Harbour looking towards Vaucluse and the city in 2000.